Dear Pop,

For as many times as I didn't want to or couldn't recognize the wisdom you've shared with me in my life, I want you to know I was always listening. Thank you for being a wonderful father to Jen and me.

Happy Father's Day!

Love,

Luke & Jen

THE TAO OF DAD

THE TAO OF DAD

The Wisdom of Fathers Near and Far

TARO GOLD

Andrews McMeel Publishing

Kansas City

*With love and appreciation
for my stepfather, David,
who always knew
the answers to my questions
and, better yet,
showed me how to find them
inside myself*

06 07 08 09 10 TWP 10 9 8 7 6 5 4 3 2 1

ISBN-13: 978-0-7407-5719-8
ISBN-10: 0-7407-5719-9

Library of Congress Control Number: 2005932199

www.andrewsmcmeel.com

Illustrations by Matthew Taylor
Book design by Lisa Martin

INTRODUCTION

My life has been blessed with a number of great dads—my father and stepfather being foremost.

Today, I believe, the importance of strong, healthy, happy men engaged in children's lives is undervalued.

Being a real dad means more than just fathering children—it means being a loving, nurturing, experienced guide on the path of life.

If we are lucky, we can count multiple dads in our lives—grandfathers, uncles, brothers, stepdads, teachers, coaches, mentors, and even friends—any male role models we look up to. All deserve to be honored, remembered, and especially emulated. We are their legacy, and the most valuable tribute we can offer them is to be the best we can be.

This little book, *The Tao of Dad*, celebrates the spirit of such noble men—the best of the best. It contains real words about real life that show us how we can be wiser, happier, if only we open our hearts and minds a little wider. It is a unique collection filled with inspiring gems of insight shared by dads around the world and across the ages.

Tao (pronounced da-oh) is a Chinese word meaning "path" or "way" and also implying "teachings" or "wisdom." *The Tao of Dad*, then, is *The Way of Great Men*, which to me represents the way of compassion, insight, and strength. It is a heritage of wisdom passed down through the generations; a natural sense of truth we all share in the depths of our hearts.

Filled with 400 inspiring and thought-provoking guideposts, the following pages hold reminders from 160 men who helped shape the lives of people in their families, communities, countries, and beyond. Some of the men in *The Tao of Dad* will be familiar to you, while others (such as dads from my family tree) you will meet for the first time. May their words remind you of cherished moments, important lessons, and hope-filled visions that your many dads have shared with you.

Let this volume be a gift to both yourself and the men you love—a heartfelt way to say, "Thank you! I'm a better person because you are in my life."

And, who knows? *The Tao of Dad* may just have the power to help you be the best you can be—so that, before you know it, someone whose life you touch will be saying the very same thing to you.

The Tao of Dad

父の道

Dream like you mean it.
—Dad

You miss 100 percent of the shots you never take.
—Wayne Gretzky

Live as if you were to die tomorrow.
Learn as if you were to live forever.
—Mahatma Gandhi

You cannot capture happiness no matter how much
you chase after it. Happiness is something that follows you;
it follows your positive actions.
—Daisaku Ikeda

What you have done for another yesterday
will be done for you today.
—Nichiren

He who controls others may be powerful,
but he who has mastered himself is mightier still.
—Lao-tzu

❧

Create your life as you would a painting.
Use a wide range of different, vivid colors.
—Grandpa

❧

The significance of a man is not in what he attains,
but rather in what he longs to attain.
—Kahlil Gibran

❧

It is not the strongest of the species that survive, nor the
most intelligent, but those most responsive to change.
—Charles Darwin

❧

You are what you think you are; you are made by your thoughts.
—Dad

Never passively accept suffering as your destiny.
—Josei Toda

The truly compassionate can avoid unhappiness; the truly wise can avoid confusion; the truly brave can avoid fear.
—Confucius

Money has never yet made anyone rich.
—Seneca

Life itself is reason for joy.
—Dad

Nothing is too difficult for him who loves.
—Cicero

Love is friendship caught on fire.
—Bruce Lee

Positive and negative impulses exist within us all. Those of us who shine brightest are not those who have no darker side but those who are fully aware of their negativity, who keep their darkness in check by increasing their light.

—Dad

No sooner said than done—so acts a man of worth.

—Quintus Ennius

Peace, like charity, begins at home.

—Franklin D. Roosevelt

Protect the purity of your mind and body—they are the vehicle of your spirit. When you continually strengthen your body and sharpen your mind, your spirit will have the power to take you wherever you wish to go.

—Grandpa

$\mathcal{I}$ simply believe that some part of the human Self or Soul is not subject to the laws of space and time.

—Carl Jung

Never seek God outside yourself.

—Great-Grandpa

Love the animals, love the plants, love everything. If you love everything, you will perceive the divine mystery in things. Once you perceive it, you will begin to comprehend it better every day. And you will come at last to adore the whole world with an all-embracing love.

—Fyodor Dostoyevsky

Passionately seek out new experiences. Develop your curiosity and imagination without limits. The day you cease to be imaginative and curious is the day you cease to be.

—Dad

$\mathcal{I}$t is not a lack of love but a lack of friendship
that makes unhappy marriages.

—Friedrich Nietzsche

🍃

$\mathcal{T}$here is no remedy for love but to love more.

—Henry David Thoreau

🍃

$\mathcal{L}$isten to the Anthem of the Dawn!
Look to this Day!
For Yesterday is but a Dream,
And Tomorrow is only a Vision;
But Today well-lived makes
Every Yesterday a Dream of Happiness,
And every Tomorrow a Vision of Hope.
Look well therefore to this Day!
Such is the Anthem of the Dawn!

—Kalidasa

One word frees us of all the weight and pain in life.
That word is Love.
—*Sophocles*

A wise man is never afraid to say "I don't know."
—*Uncle Miller*

The difference between what we do and what we are
capable of doing would suffice to solve most problems.
—*Mahatma Gandhi*

A day without laughter is a day wasted.
—*Grandpa*

When you struggle to reach for something you don't know,
that's where the most interesting stuff is.
—*Herbie Hancock*

$\mathcal{Y}$our family is not the world—the world is your family.
—Dad

🍃

$\mathcal{E}$ven
After all this time,
The sun never says to the earth,
"You owe me."
Look at what happens
With a love like that;
It lights the whole sky.
—Hafez

🍃

$\mathcal{C}$omplaints erase good fortune.
Gratitude builds happiness for all eternity.
—Daisaku Ikeda

🍃

$\mathcal{L}$ook within. Within is the fountain of good,
and it will ever bubble up, if thou wilt ever dig.
—Marcus Aurelius

9

When I'm working on a problem,
I never think about beauty. I think only
how to solve the problem. But when I have
finished, if the solution is not beautiful,
I know it is wrong.
—R. Buckminster Fuller

Talking to your heart is good;
listening to your heart is better.
—Grandpa

Over-seriousness is a warning sign
of mediocrity and bureaucratic thinking.
People who are truly committed to
mastery and high performance are
secure enough to lighten up.
—Michael J. Gelb

Do even small things in a big way.
—Dad

Sometime in the near future most people will be insane,
and when they encounter someone who is not insane,
they will persecute him and accuse him of being
insane because he is not like them.
—Grandpa

All that evil requires to succeed is for
good people to do nothing.
—Benjamin Franklin

Exemplify thoughtfulness and kindness in everything you do.
—Uncle Miller

Failure is success if we learn from it.
—Malcolm Forbes

Perhaps the most important revelation
in life is to recognize your own worth.
—Dad

The kingdom of heaven is within you.

—Jesus

Undoubtedly it is around the family and home that all
the greatest virtues, the most dominating virtues of human
society are created, strengthened, and maintained.

—Winston Churchill

When people talk to us about others, we call them "chatty."
When people talk to us about themselves, we call them "boring."
When people talk to us about ourselves, we call them "brilliant."

—Grandpa

May you find,
Before your end,
The pure deep love,
Of one true good friend.

—Great-Grandpa

Education is the most powerful weapon
one can use to change the world.
—Nelson Mandela

Power is only important as an instrument
for service to the powerless.
—Lech Walesa

If you want others to be happy,
practice compassion.
If you want yourself to be happy,
practice compassion.
—the Dalai Lama

The distance between your dreams and your reality is
always traversable. If you can dream it, you can make it so.
—Daisaku Ikeda

To make a great dream come true, the first requirement
is a great capacity to dream; the second is persistence.
—Cesar Chavez

Agreement is the process of changing people's
minds—other people's, of course.
—S. I. Hayakawa

Think deeper. Look closer. Nothing is as it seems.
—Dad

A true leader, a true man of action,
acts subconsciously in a moment of crisis, and then
thinks of the reasons for his actions later.
—Jawaharlal Nehru

Avoid looking for shortcuts on
a direct path or risk losing your way.
—Grandpa

Who you are thunders so greatly that I cannot
hear what you say to the contrary.
—Ralph Waldo Emerson

Doubt is not a pleasant mental state,
but certainty is a ridiculous one.
—Voltaire

Go confidently in the direction of your dreams.
Live the life you have imagined.
—Henry David Thoreau

Little by little, one travels far.
—J. R. R. Tolkien

To teach another something is like oiling the
wheels of a heavy cart so that they will turn.
—Nichiren

I hear and I forget. I see and I remember.
I do and I understand.

—Confucius

There is no greater aid on the path to
enlightenment than a true friend.

—Dad

When the effective leader is finished with his work,
the people say it happened naturally.

—Lao-tzu

No matter how difficult your state of life may be
at any given time, whatever your circumstances, always
do your best, and keep going. Always go forward.

—Christopher Reeve

Always follow your heart.

—Uncle Miller

Tenderness and kindness are not signs of weakness or despair;
they are manifestations of strength and resolution.

—Kahlil Gibran

Words left unsaid form bricks in the heart,
and feelings left unfelt build them into walls.

—Dad

The secret of health in both mind and body is not to mourn
for the past, worry about the future, or anticipate troubles,
but to live in the present moment wisely and earnestly.

—Shakyamuni

To love excellence is to love the gods.

—Aristotle

Those who are victorious plan effectively,
and change decisively. They are like a great river that
maintains its course, but adjusts its flow. They have form,
but are formless. They are skilled in both planning
and adapting, and need not fear the result of
a thousand battles: For they win in advance,
defeating those who have already lost.

—Sun-tzu

A truth that's told with bad intent
beats all the lies you can invent.

—William Blake

To learn from your mistakes, you must start
by admitting that you made them.

—Dad

Physical force is temporary, as the body is transitory.
But spiritual power is permanent, as the spirit is everlasting.
—Mahatma Gandhi

People are quick to blame chance for their failures
and accidents, and quicker still to take personal responsibility
for all the good that comes their way.
—Dad

Thinkers do not accept the inevitable;
they turn their efforts toward changing it.
—Paramhansa Yogananda

Appreciation is what makes people truly human.
—Daisaku Ikeda

Money may be the husk of many things, but not the kernel.
It brings you food, not appetite; medicine, not health;
acquaintances, not friends; servitude, not faithfulness;
days of leisure, not peace and happiness.

—Henrik Ibsen

When one no longer seeks to be better,
one no longer seeks to be.

—Dad

Just when the caterpillar thought the world was ending,
the caterpillar became a butterfly.

—Grandpa

There is no teacher better than adversity. Every defeat,
every heartbreak, every loss, contains its own seed, its own
lesson on how to improve your performance next time.

—Malcolm X

One thing you can never give too much of is gratitude.

—Dad

Use what talents you possess: The woods would be very
quiet if no birds there sang except those that sang best.

—Henry Van Dyke

We are primarily on this earth not to see through
one another, but to see one another through.

—Peter De Vries

The only perfect perception we have is hindsight.

—Uncle Miller

Knowledge, ability, and experience are of little avail in reaching high success if kindness is lacking. Kindness is the one passport that will be accepted without question in every land, in every office, in every home, in every heart in the world. For nothing commends itself so well as kindness.

—George D. Powers

True religion is real living; living with all one's soul, with all one's goodness, all one's honesty.

—Albert Einstein

Sometimes it's better to be filled with questions rather than hold all the answers. The true beauty of life is in the questions.

—Grandpa

Poverty of goods is easily cured; poverty of soul, impossible.

—Michel de Montaigne

Love looks through a telescope;
jealousy through a microscope.
—Josh Billings

Honesty is the first chapter in the book of wisdom.
—Thomas Jefferson

We listen too much to the sounds of machines and too
little to the sounds of nature. The greatest sound of all—
and to me it is a sound—is the sound of silence.
—Great-Grandpa

Parenting can only be learned by people who have no children.
—Bill Cosby

The measure of a man's true nature is how he would
behave if he knew he never would be found out.
—Grandpa

Is war the inescapable fate of humanity? No. War is the symptom of defeat. Though people think they can use military force for their own purposes, in the end they always find themselves its victims. For once war begins, the barbaric, devilish nature residing in our innermost beings is unleashed and runs riot.

—Daisaku Ikeda

Quality means doing it right when no one is looking.

—Henry Ford

Revenge is the way ignorant people express anguish.

—Grandpa

To hold a man down, you have to stay down with him.

—Booker T. Washington

In matters of conscience, the law of majority has no place.

—Mahatma Gandhi

Lose your wealth and you've lost nothing.
Lose your health and you've lost something.
Lose your character and you've lost everything.
—Ben Lapadula

Happiness is a practice. It is a habit.
—Dad

Burn the firewood of earthly desires and
reveal enlightenment within its flames.
—Nichiren

Victorious warriors win first and then go to war, while
defeated warriors go to war first and then seek to win.
—Sun-tzu

Real integrity stays in place whether
the test is adversity or prosperity.
—Charles Swindoll

How come people never have time to do it right
the first time but always have time to do it over?
—Dad

To thine own self be true,
and it must follow,
as the night the day,
thou canst not then be false to any man.
—William Shakespeare

Morality is always the product of terror; its chains
are fashioned by those who dare not trust others,
because they dare not trust themselves, to walk in liberty.
—Aldous Huxley

There is something more horrible than hoodlums, churls, and vipers, and that is knaves with moral justification for their cause.
—Thomas Moore

Moralizing and morals are two entirely different things and are always found in entirely different people.
—Don Herold

Those who have knowledge of the natural way do not train themselves in cunning, whilst those who use cunning to rule their lives, and the lives of others, are not knowledgeable of natural happiness.
—Lao-tzu

Old friends go away, new friends appear. It is just like the days. An old day passes, a new day arrives. The important thing is to make it all meaningful: meaningful friends—meaningful days.
—the Dalai Lama

A child cannot be spoiled by things.
Children can only be spoiled by people. It is not what
you give a child; it is how you raise a child.

—Grandpa

Nonviolence is the greatest virtue, cowardice the greatest vice.
Nonviolence springs from love, cowardice from hate.
Nonviolence suffers. Cowardice inflicts suffering.

—Mahatma Gandhi

True merit, like a river, the deeper it is, the less noise it makes.

—Edward Frederick Halifax

An artist is anyone who takes pride in doing a job well.

—Uncle Miller

Humility is the solid foundation of all virtues.

—Confucius

Be wise and dignified like the swan: he maintains
his composure, staying unruffled on the surface
while always paddling like crazy underneath.

—Daisaku Ikeda

Never waste your time with a friend who does not help you
better yourself, who only helps distract you from feelings
of loneliness. When the true friend you seek is not found
easily, however, you become impatient. You fill the gap with
anyone who comes along, idling your time with meaningless
interaction, missing out on the most valuable time and
experience you could have spent alone. Instead, use your
solitude to create the deepest inner character, build
the strongest heart, and blossom into the person you
once dreamed of finding. Having begun this hardest
of work within, you will naturally attract a friend who
can help you better yourself from without.

—Dad

The impression somehow prevails that the true believer,
particularly the religious individual, is a humble person.
The truth is that the surrendering and humbling
of the self breeds pride and arrogance.
—Eric Hoffer

It is important that man dreams, but it is perhaps
equally important that he can laugh at his own dreams.

—Lin Yutang

When I do good, I feel good.
When I do bad, I feel bad. And that's my religion.

—Abraham Lincoln

Life isn't about finding yourself. Life is about creating yourself.

—Grandpa

Say not, "I have found the truth," but rather, "I have found *a*
truth." Say not, "I have found the path of the soul." Say rather,
"I have met the soul walking upon my path." For the soul walks
upon all paths. The soul walks not upon a line, neither does it grow
like a reed. The soul unfolds itself, like a lotus of countless petals.

—Kahlil Gibran

As long as there is poverty in the world I can never be totally rich. As long as people are afflicted with debilitating diseases I can never be totally healthy. I can never be what I ought to be until you are what you ought to be.

—Martin Luther King, Jr.

Live with hope. Nothing is stronger than hope. Happiness belongs to those who never despair, no matter what happens.

—Daisaku Ikeda

It is every man's obligation to put back into the world at least the equivalent of what he takes out of it.

—Albert Einstein

Gaining the faith of others is of little importance. Truly, deeply believing in yourself is what matters most. When you completely believe in yourself, life will reward you with more joy than you ever imagined.

—Dad

We make a living by what we get,
but we make a life by what we give.
—Winston Churchill

It is not the critic who counts, not the man who points out how the strong man stumbled or where the doer of deeds could have done better. The credit belongs to the man who is actually in the arenas; whose face is marred by dust and sweat and blood, who strives valiantly; who errs and comes up short again and again; who knows the great enthusiasm, the great devotions, and spends himself in a worthy cause; who at the best knows in the end the triumph of high achievements; and who at the worst, if he fails, at least fails while daring greatly; so that his place shall never be with those cold and timid souls who know neither defeat nor victory.
—Theodore Roosevelt

Be good at what you do. Don't worry about being different. Being good is different enough.
—Great-Grandpa

Iron rusts from disuse; water loses its purity from stagnation.
So does inaction sap vigor from the mind.
—Leonardo da Vinci

🍃

The growth of the human spirit has not kept pace with the times.
—Dad

🍃

Individuality is freedom lived.
—John Dos Passos

🍃

All greatness of character is dependent on individuality.
The man who has no other existence than that which he
partakes in common with all around him will never
have any other than an existence of mediocrity.
—James Fenimore Cooper

🍃

Nourish your spirit every day.
—Dad

And this I believe: that the free, exploring mind of the individual is the most valuable thing in all the world. And this I would fight for: the freedom of the mind to take any direction it wishes, undirected. And this I must fight against: any idea, religion, or government which limits or destroys the individual.

—John Steinbeck

Respect others in their views and demand that they respect yours. Trouble no one about his religion. Love your life, purify your life, beautify all things in your life. Seek to make your life of service to people.

—Tecumseh

Gratitude is a quality similar to electricity: it must be produced and discharged and used up in order to exist at all.

—William Faulkner

As we express our gratitude, we must never forget that the highest appreciation is not to utter words, but to live by them.

—John Fitzgerald Kennedy

Lies can hide the past and may fix the present but will destroy the future.

—Grandpa

Plan for the future, because that is where you are going to spend the rest of your life.

—Mark Twain

My own mind is my own church.

—Thomas Paine

One who performs good deeds is certain to prosper.

—Nichiren

$\mathcal{E}$nlighten the people generally, and tyranny and oppressions of body and mind will vanish like spirits at the dawn of day.
—Thomas Jefferson

$\mathcal{S}$olitude is misunderstood. Most people are taught to avoid it, to be ashamed of it, to regret it. With the correct view, however, time spent alone becomes the springboard for all meaningful time spent with others. It is in solitude that the foundation for all goodness in one's life is built.
—Dad

$\mathcal{Y}$ou all laugh at me because I am different.
I laugh at you because you're all the same.
—Vick Imbornoni

$\mathcal{I}$t's a shallow life that doesn't give a person a few scars.
—Garrison Keillor

What you don't know may hurt you,
but it will certainly amuse a lot of people.

—Uncle Miller

🍃

As long as we remain preoccupied with our own troubles,
as long as we allow ourselves to blindly follow the impulsive
dictates of our minds, our sufferings will continue. We must
master our minds rather than let our minds be our
master, consciously redirecting our thoughts in a
positive direction and helping others do the same.

—Daisaku Ikeda

🍃

All persons ought to endeavor to follow
what is true and not what is established.

—Aristotle

🍃

God has no religion.

—Mahatma Gandhi

$\mathcal{I}$t is easy in the world to live after the world's opinion;
but the great man is he who in the midst of the crowd keeps
with perfect sweetness the independence of solitude.

—Ralph Waldo Emerson

$\mathcal{A}$ human being is a part of the whole, called by us
"Universe," a part limited in time and space. He experiences
himself, his thoughts and feelings, as something separated
from the rest—a kind of optical delusion of his consciousness.
This delusion is a kind of prison for us, restricting us to our
personal desires and to affection for a few persons nearest
to us. Our task must be to free ourselves from this prison
by widening our circle of compassion to embrace all living
creatures and the whole of nature in its beauty. Nobody
is able to achieve this completely, but the striving
for such achievement is in itself a part of liberation
and a foundation for inner security.

—Albert Einstein

Let go of whatever brings you down.
—Dad

The function of education is to teach one to think
intensively and critically. Intelligence plus character—
that is the goal of true education.
—Martin Luther King, Jr.

Discover your passion and follow it with all your heart.
—Grandpa

Being deeply loved gives you strength;
loving deeply gives you courage.
—Lao-tzu

The People are the ultimate guardians of their own liberty.
—Thomas Jefferson

The individual has always
had to struggle to keep from
being overwhelmed by the tribe.
To be your own man is hard
business. If you try it, you will
be lonely often, and sometimes
frightened. But no price is too
high to pay for the privilege
of owning yourself.
—Rudyard Kipling

Art is one of life's greatest gifts.
It gives much and asks nothing in return.
—Grandpa

I hope that all mankind will at length, as they call
themselves reasonable creatures, have reason and sense enough
to settle their differences without cutting throats; for in my
opinion there never was a good war or a bad peace.
—Benjamin Franklin

Question habit. Eliminate negativity. Purify your life.

—Dad

🍂

The law is not the private property of lawyers, nor is justice the exclusive province of judges and juries. In the final analysis, true justice is not a matter of courts and law books, but of a commitment in each of us to liberty and mutual respect.

—Jimmy Carter

🍂

Change always comes, no matter what. Change is constant and rarely controllable. Whether you grow with change or are defeated by it, however, is completely within your control.

—Great-Grandpa

🍂

Ignorance is always afraid of change.

—Jawaharlal Nehru

To the questions in your life, you are the only answer.
To the problems in your life, you are the only solution.
—Grandpa

Forget insults and injuries; never forget kindnesses.
—Confucius

Every story has three sides—yours, mine, and the facts.
—Dad

The great enemy of the truth is very often not the lie—
deliberate, contrived, and dishonest—but the myth—
persistent, persuasive, and unrealistic.
—John Fitzgerald Kennedy

Always live true to yourself.
—Josei Toda

There is no birth of consciousness without pain.
—Carl Jung

One of the deep secrets of life is that all that
is really worth doing is what we do for others.
—Lewis Carroll

Duplicity leads only to misery.
—Dad

Your children are not your children.
They are the sons and daughters of
Life's longing for itself.
They come through you but not from you,
And though they are with you,
Yet they belong not to you.
—Kahlil Gibran

All the happiness in the world comes from
thinking of others; all the suffering in the world
comes from thinking only of oneself.
—Shantiveda

Controversy is an inevitable partner of greatness.
No one who challenges the established order is free of it.
Controversy is often a testament to noble work, and
accompanies the lives of all truly great humanitarians.
—Lawrence Carter

The victory of culture is a victory for peace. A true victory
for peace can never be obtained by guns. Culture and music
are our "weapons." Government is concerned with power;
economics is concerned with profit and loss. But culture
profoundly touches people in the depths of their lives.
Music speaks to people's hearts and brings them closer together.
—Daisaku Ikeda

Remember that change is opportunity's nickname.
—Grandpa

A price must be paid for success. Those who have reached
the summits have invariably worked harder and longer,
studied and planned more assiduously, practiced more
self-denial, and overcome more difficulties than
those of us who have not risen so far.
—B. C. Forbes

I skate where the game is going to be, not where it has been.
—Wayne Gretzky

If we listened to our intellect, we'd never find friendship.
We'd never have love. We'd never go into business.
We'd be pessimistic. Well, that's nonsense. You've got to jump
off cliffs all the time and build your wings on the way down.
—Ray Bradbury

No man is hurt but by himself.
—Diogenes

One of the greatest steps a man can take is
the one he takes to meet another person halfway.
—Uncle Miller

When praised highly by others, one feels that
there is no hardship one cannot bear. Such is
the courage that springs from words of praise.
—Nichiren

We can live without religion,
but we cannot survive without affection.
—the Dalai Lama

Live your life that the fear of death can never enter your heart. Prepare a noble death song for the day when you go over the great divide. When your time comes to die, be not like those whose hearts are filled with fear of death, so that when their time comes they weep and pray for a little more time to live their lives over again in a different way.

Sing your death song, and die like a hero going home.

—Tecumseh

When shadows appear in your life, look for the light, for shadows cannot exist without light.

—Dad

Find the good. It's all around you.

Find it, showcase it, and you'll start believing in it.

—Jesse Owens

Once upon a time, a large, rough samurai went to see a small, gentle monk, hoping to acquire the secrets of life. "Monk," he said, in a voice accustomed to total obedience. "Teach me about heaven and hell."

The little monk looked up in silence. After a moment, the monk said with disdain, "Teach *you* about heaven and hell? I couldn't teach you about anything. You're dirty. You smell. Your blade is rusty. You're a disgrace, an embarrassment to the samurai class. Get out of my sight at once. I can't stand you!"

The samurai was furious. A red flush spread over his face as he began to shake from anger, speechless with rage. Quickly, he pulled out his sword and raised it above his head, preparing to kill the little monk with one swift blow.

"That's hell," said the monk.

The samurai was stunned. What compassion and surrender of this gentle man who had risked his life to give this teaching about hell. He slowly lowered his sword, filled with gratitude. For reasons he could not explain, his heart became suddenly peaceful, appreciative, and loving.

"And that's heaven," said the monk.

Patience is the companion of wisdom.
—Saint Augustine

No one can harm the man
who does himself no wrong.
—Saint John Chrysostom

Find humor every day.
Laughter keeps the spirit young.
—Grandpa

The more freedom we enjoy,
the greater the responsibility we bear,
toward others as well as ourselves.
—Oscar Arias Sánchez

The best victory is when your opponent surrenders
of his own accord before there are any actual hostilities.
It is always best to win without fighting.

—Sun-tzu

You've got to be honest; if you can fake that, you've got it made.

—George Burns

Do not be too moral. You may cheat
yourself out of much life. Aim above morality.

—Henry David Thoreau

Rather than trying to become a man of success,
try to become a man of value.

—Albert Einstein

If you have built castles in the air, your work need not be lost;
that is where they should be. Now put the foundations under them.

—Henry David Thoreau

*F*irst they ignore you; then they laugh at you;
then they fight you; then you win.

—Mahatma Gandhi

*C*herish, honor, and respect yourself.

—Dad

*E*verything that I understand,
I understand only because I love.

—Leo Tolstoy

*T*here is nothing more yielding than water, yet when
acting on the solid and strong, its gentleness and fluidity
have no equal in anything. The weak can overcome the strong,
and the supple overcome the hard. Although this is known
far and wide, few put it into practice in their lives.

—Lao-tzu

$\mathcal{J}$nstead of thinking "I should," think "I shall."

—*Grandpa*

$\mathcal{J}$t is a paradoxical but profoundly true and
important principle of life that the most likely way to
reach a goal is by aiming not at the goal itself but
at some more ambitious goal beyond it.

—*Arnold Toynbee*

$\mathcal{T}$he important thing is that we find our happiness within,
for we can thereby help everyone around us to do the same.

—*Daisaku Ikeda*

$\mathcal{T}$he moon and beyond is not very far to go.
Greater distances have yet to be journeyed
within our own hearts and minds.

—*Great-Grandpa*

Everything you've learned in school as "obvious" becomes
less and less obvious as you begin to study the universe.
For example, there are no solids in the universe. There's not
even a suggestion of a solid. There are no absolute continuums.
There are no surfaces. There are no straight lines.
—R. Buckminster Fuller

There is nothing like returning to a place that remains
unchanged to see the ways in which you yourself have changed.
—Nelson Mandela

This is my simple religion. There is no need for temples,
no need for complication. One's own mind, one's own
heart is the temple, and loving-kindness is the philosophy.
—the Dalai Lama

Don't worry about the world coming to an end today.
It's already tomorrow in Australia.
—Charles M. Schulz

Respect yourself, and others will respect you.
— Confucius

Carefully observe which way your heart directs you,
then choose that way with all your might.
— Grandpa

Nearly all marriages, even happy ones, are mistakes
in the sense that almost certainly in a more perfect world,
or even with a little more care in this very imperfect one, both
partners might have found more suitable mates. Your real
soul-mate, however, is the one to whom you are actually married.
— J. R. R. Tolkien

Along the path of our happiness we find the
learning for which we have chosen this lifetime.
— Richard Bach

Wise people deserve to be called so because they are not carried away by the eight winds: prosperity, decline, honor, disgrace, praise, criticism, pleasure, and suffering. They are neither elated by prosperity nor grieved by decline. The heavenly gods will surely protect one who is unbending before the eight winds.

—Nichiren

Your intentions create your reality.

—Dad

Act as if what you do makes a difference. It does.

—William James

We must develop and maintain the capacity to forgive. He who is devoid of the power to forgive is devoid of the power to love.

—Martin Luther King, Jr.

Always forgive your enemies—
nothing annoys them so much.
—Oscar Wilde

War does not determine who is right—only who is left.
—Bertrand Russell

It is the habit of every aggressor nation
to claim that it is acting on the defensive.
—Jawaharlal Nehru

The power of accurate observation is commonly
called cynicism by those who have not got it.
—George Bernard Shaw

The things you are most afraid of doing
are usually the most worthwhile.
—Dad

What the world needs is more geniuses with humility,
there are so few of us left.

—Oscar Levant

Modesty is the art of drawing attention to
whatever it is you are being humble about.

—Uncle Miller

Expand your boundaries beyond your comfort zone.
Open your heart and mind each day wider than before, beyond
your imagination. Taste life in all its wondrous diversity.
Be courageous. Venture directly into the fog of the unknown.
The unfamiliar may feel uncomfortable or frightening—but
when you clear your vision from stains of habit and false
knowledge, you can see right through it. Fear of the unknown
is nothing but a grand illusion. The truth is that only in
uncharted territory will you discover your true self. Only there
will you find the lasting treasures of freedom, love, and joy.

—Dad

Love looks not with the eyes, but with the mind,
And therefore is winged Cupid painted blind.
—William Shakespeare

Success in life has nothing to do with what you gain
or accomplish for yourself. It's what you do for others.
—Danny Thomas

Freedom is not the chance to do as you please.
Freedom is the opportunity to do what is right.
—Peter Marshall

Increase your joy by doing the good you wish to
have done to you. Decrease your suffering by refusing
to do the bad that has been done to you.
—Daisaku Ikeda

Joy increases as you give it, and diminishes as you try to keep it for yourself. In giving it, you will accumulate a deposit of joy greater than you ever believed possible.

—Norman Vincent Peale

To become an excellent leader, you have to abandon addiction to praise from above and flattery from below. The excellent leader leads least. He studies the distinctive skills and natural inclinations of both those above and those below, and he directs their attention to accomplish what is required to benefit all. When this has been done, all declare they have been part of a worthwhile purpose.

—Lao-tzu

Try to learn something about everything and everything about something.

—T. H. Huxley

If you try to be like someone else, who will be like you?

—Grandpa

If a man does not keep pace
with his companions, perhaps
it is because he hears a different
drummer. Let him step to the
music which he hears,
however measured or far away.
—Henry David Thoreau

Each human being is bred
with a unique set of potentials
that yearn to be fulfilled as
surely as the acorn yearns
to become the oak within it.
—Aristotle

People deserve to have more than two little
decades between the ages of twenty and forty.
—Great-Grandpa

The greatest journey you can take is the journey inward.
—Dad

Each one of us contains multitudes.
—Walt Whitman

We carry inside us the wonders we seek outside us.
—Sir Thomas Browne

All that we achieve and all that we fail to
achieve is the direct result of our own thoughts.
—James Allen

We must become the change we wish to see.
—Mahatma Gandhi

The greatest men who have ever walked this earth
are those who made the greatest changes in their hearts.
—Dad

We cannot teach people anything;
we can only help them discover it within themselves.
—Galileo Galilei

❧

Whenever a radical new concept is proposed,
people don't believe it is possible. But soon they begin
to hope it is possible. Eventually they realize it is definitely
possible. And once it has been achieved, everyone
wonders why it was not accomplished long ago.
—Uncle Miller

❧

The only way to help oneself is to help others.
—Kahlil Gibran

❧

Make your spirit flexible, and nothing
will ever bend you out of shape.
—Dad

$\mathcal{A}$ loving heart is the truest wisdom.
—Charles Dickens

$\mathcal{P}$eople will forget what you say and do, but they
will always remember how you made them feel.
—Grandpa

$\mathcal{B}$e not simply good; be good for something.
—Henry David Thoreau

$\mathcal{I}$ am still learning, forever learning.
—Michelangelo

$\mathcal{B}$e you. Be open. Be different. Be unexpected.
Be anything but ordinary.
—Dad

Champions know that success is inevitable; that
there is no such thing as failure, only feedback. They know
that the best way to forecast the future is to create it.
—Michael J. Gelb

🍃

Even if you're on the right track, you'll get
run over if you just sit there.
—Arthur Godfrey

🍃

The key to wisdom is this—constant and frequent
questioning. For by doubting we are led to question
and by questioning we arrive at the truth.
—Peter Abelard

🍃

Whatever you do, or dream you can, begin it.
Boldness has genius and power and magic in it.
—Johann Wolfgang von Goethe

The wise know how to disagree without being disagreeable.
—Uncle Miller

He who opens a school door, closes a prison.
—Victor Hugo

No matter how long and bitter the winter may be,
spring always follows. This is the law of the universe, the
law of life. The same applies to us. If we seem to be weathering
an endless winter, we mustn't abandon hope. As long as
we have hope, spring will come without fail.
—Daisaku Ikeda

Men of honor and integrity will always choose to be
correct and alone rather than wrong and with the majority.
—Dad

Civilization is a movement and not a condition,
a voyage and not a harbor.
—Arnold Toynbee

If you did not know your age, what age would you feel you are?
—Grandpa

Behind every successful man stands a surprised mother-in-law.
—Hubert Humphrey

The most powerful, self-affirming love includes
loving those who brought you unhappiness.
—Dad

Any fool can make a rule, and any fool will mind it.
—Henry David Thoreau

One should not be intimidated by the fact that so many
people hold false beliefs. Nor does the truth of a belief depend
on whether it has been held for a long or short time.
The point is simply whether or not it conforms with reason.
—Nichiren

Words that are strictly true often seem paradoxical.
—Lao-tzu

The opposite of love is not hate, it is indifference. The opposite of art is not ugliness, it is indifference. The opposite of faith is not heresy, it is indifference. The opposite of life is not death, it is indifference. Indifference, to me, is the epitome of evil.
—Elie Wiesel

Keep true to the dreams of thy youth.
—Friedrich von Schiller

Nothing strengthens authority as much as silence.
—Leonardo da Vinci

Men's natures are all alike; it is their habits that carry them far apart.
—Confucius

Extraordinary people swim out into the middle of the vast ocean. Ordinary people remain seated safely on the shore. Take chances. Get wet.

—Dad

When you rise in the morning, give thanks for the light, for your life, for your strength. Give thanks for your food and for the joy of living. If you see no reason to give thanks, the fault lies only in yourself.

—Tecumseh

Those who make peaceful revolution impossible will make violent revolution inevitable.

—John Fitzgerald Kennedy

If you wish your talents to be known, acknowledge other people's talents.

—Grandpa

The art of life lies in a constant readjustment to our surroundings.
—Okakura Kakuzo

I believe in looking reality straight in the eye and denying it.
—Garrison Keillor

The state of the world is no worse today than
it was one hundred years ago. It only seems worse
now because news coverage is more advanced.
—Great-Grandpa

The policy of being too cautious is the greatest risk of all.
—Jawaharlal Nehru

He who has hope has everything.
—Dad

❦

Knowledge is like a double-edged sword. It may be
turned to dangerous uses if it is not properly handled.
—Wu Ting-fang

❦

Besides the noble art of getting things done,
there is a nobler art of leaving things undone.
The wisdom of life consists in eliminating nonessentials.
—Lin Yutang

❦

A wrongdoer is often a man who has left something undone,
not always one who has done something.
—Marcus Aurelius

❦

Your true friends are your true family.
—Grandpa

In a crazy world, only the crazy are sane.
—Akira Kurosawa

Nothing is so firmly believed as that which we least know.
—Michel de Montaigne

If I have a thousand ideas and only
one turns out to be good, I am satisfied.
—Alfred Nobel

Handle your family as you would handle fine china—very gently.
—Grandpa

Better than a thousand heads bowing in prayer
is giving peace to a single heart by a single act.
—Mahatma Gandhi

Most important is what is said, not who says it.

—Dad

🍃

Anger is a great force. If you control it, it can be
transmuted into a power which can move the whole world.

—Sri Swami Sivananda

🍃

Real love is not two people clinging to each other;
it can only be fostered between two strong people secure
in their individuality. A shallow person will have only shallow
relationships. If you want to experience real love, it is
important to first sincerely develop a strong self-identity.

—Daisaku Ikeda

🍃

Everyone is an actor performing the play of life.
It is we who write the scenario and perform our own script.
As such, we have the power to change anything in our lives.

—Pascual Olivera

Success is to be measured not so much by the
position that one has reached in life, as by the
obstacles one has overcome trying to succeed.
—Booker T. Washington

Achieving action through inaction is a sign of genius.
—Dad

The oneness of human beings is the basic
ethical thread that holds us together.
—Muhammad Yunus

Once upon a time, a boy dreamt that he was a butterfly,
fluttering happily like a butterfly. He was conscious only
of his happiness as a butterfly, unaware that he was a boy.
Suddenly he awakened, and there he was, a boy. Now he
does not know whether the butterfly is a dream of the boy,
or whether the boy is a dream of the butterfly.
—Chuang-tzu

The joys of parents are often kept secret,
as are their griefs and fears.
—Francis Bacon

Winners don't do different things. They do things differently.
—Shiv Kera

Blossoms are scattered by the wind and the wind cares nothing,
but the blossoms of the heart no wind can touch.
—Yoshida Kenko

Follow your passion, and you will find joy.
—Dad

If you give a man a fish, he will have a single meal.
If you teach him how to fish, he will eat all his life.
—Kwan-tzu

75

$\mathcal{I}$t is said that an enemy can teach you more than a friend. A great friend, however, can help you learn even more than an enemy, for a great friend has the wisdom to see from the perspective of an enemy as well as a comrade.

—Grandpa

Many evil forces are vanquished by a single great truth.

—Nichiren

Happiness is not something ready made.
It comes from your own actions.

—the Dalai Lama

$\mathcal{I}$f you want to be successful, avoid lying about yourself and be cautious when telling the truth about others.

—Uncle Miller

Many people think of changing the world,
but few think of changing themselves.
—Leo Tolstoy

Each evening as you finish your day, ask yourself if
you have done all you could this day to better yourself.
—Dad

Awards become corroded; friends gather no dust.
—Jesse Owens

Don't be in a hurry to condemn because he doesn't
do what you do or think as you think or as fast. There was
a time when you didn't know what you know today.
—Malcolm X

The more laws that are written, the more criminals are produced.
—Lao-tzu

Find yourself, and then never let go.
—Grandpa

When your determination is set, everything moves
in the direction of your heart, whether positive or negative.
For example, if you think "This is never going to work out,"
then at that instant every cell in your being will be deflated,
giving up the fight. Everything will then move in the
direction of failure. On the other hand, the moment
you resolve to be victorious, every nerve and fiber in your
being immediately orients itself toward your success.
—Daisaku Ikeda

True love gives three times as much as it receives.
—Great-Grandpa

In waking a tiger, use a long stick.
—Mao Zedong

78

Anger itself does more harm than
the condition that aroused it.
—Dad

All things entail the timing of rising and falling.
You must be able to discern this.
—Miyamoto Musashi

There are a few ways to distribute family income,
all of them unsatisfactory.
—Grandpa

Everything has its beauty but not everyone sees it.
—Confucius

What is true cannot die.
—Dad

$\mathcal{N}$o matter how deep you analyze
something, you ultimately have to
rely on your intuition. And when
it comes down to it, you really
won't know what's going to
happen until you do it.

—Konosuke Matsushita

$\mathcal{O}$riginality is the essence
of true scholarship. Creativity
is the soul of the true scholar.

—Benjamin Nnamdi Azikiwe

$\mathcal{E}$very now and then go away, have a little relaxation; for when
you come back to your work, your judgment will be surer.
To remain constantly at work will cause you to lose power of
judgment. When you go some distance away, then your work
appears smaller, and more of it can be taken in at a glance,
so a lack of harmony or proportion is more readily seen.

—Leonardo da Vinci

One's art is a mirror of one's mind.
—Grandpa

You can tell whether a man is clever by his answers.
You can tell whether a man is wise by his questions.
—Naguib Mahfouz

One who runs away from difficulty exposes himself
to danger more than one who confronts it head-on.
—Dad

There are immediate costs and risks to action. They are far less,
however, than the long-range risks of comfortable inaction.
—John Fitzgerald Kennedy

If we wish to cultivate true democracy, we cannot afford to be
intolerant. Intolerance reveals a lack of faith in one's own cause.
—Mahatma Gandhi

Peace is not a relationship of nations.
It is a condition of mind brought about by a serenity of the soul.
Lasting peace can come only to peaceful people.
—Jawaharlal Nehru

If liberty means anything at all, it means the
right to tell people what they do not want to hear.
—George Orwell

Always speak as you act, and act as you speak.
—Dad

We all have dreams. But to make your dreams
into reality, it takes the greatest of determination,
dedication, self-discipline, and effort.
—Jesse Owens

A perception, sudden as blinking, that subject and
object are one will lead to a deeply mysterious understanding;
and by this understanding you will awaken to the truth.
—Huang Po

Though bitter, good medicine cures illness.
Though it may hurt, loyal criticism has beneficial effects.
—Sima Qian

Adversity gives birth to greatness.
The greater challenges and difficulties we face,
the greater our opportunities for growth and success.
—Daisaku Ikeda

Continually reinvent yourself.
—Dad

Imagination is more important than knowledge.
—Albert Einstein

Imagination: the supreme delight of the
immortal and the immature.
—Vladimir Nabokov

Better than a thousand days of study
is one day with a great teacher.
—Grandpa

We are a strand in the web of life. Whatever we do to the web,
we do to ourselves. All things are connected.
—Chief Seattle

Even the treasures of the entire universe cannot
equal the value of a single human life.
—Nichiren

It is not true that we have only one life to live; if we can read, we can live as many more lives and as many kinds of lives as we wish.
—S. I. Hayakawa

We are what we repeatedly do.
Excellence, then, is not an act but a habit.
—Aristotle

Divisions are imaginary lines drawn by small minds.
—Paramhansa Yogananda

You can never love yourself too much.
—Dad

Clay is molded to make a vessel, but the importance of the vessel lies in the empty space within. Thus, taking advantage of what is, we recognize the importance of what is not.
—Lao-tzu

If you know the adversary and know yourself,
you need not fear a hundred battles.

—Sun-tzu

When a man does only what is required of him,
he is but a slave. Only when a man does more than
is required of him is he a truly free man.

—Grandpa

In an archery contest, when the prize is earthenware, a
contestant shoots with skill. When the prize is a belt buckle,
he becomes hesitant, and when the prize is pure gold he
becomes nervous and confused. There is no difference as to
his skill but, because there is something he desires, he allows
outward considerations to weigh on his mind. Those who
consider external things important become weak within.

—Chuang-tzu

*I*nspiration generates inspiration.
It gives of itself to whatever it touches.
—Paramhansa Yogananda

*L*ove all, trust few, do wrong to none.
—William Shakespeare

*A*nything truly revolutionary is created by a few
who see what is true and are willing to live according
to that truth; but to discover what is true demands freedom
from tradition, which means freedom from fear.
—Jiddu Krishnamurti

*G*iving vision to his staff and helping them achieve it is
what leadership is all about. The time of having one hero in
the company is over. The role of leadership today is to form
a cooperative tie that binds employees happily together.
—Bae Soonhoon

$\mathcal{W}$hen you look for truth outside yourself,
it gets further away.

—Dad

No matter how fortunate you are now or how
fortunate you become, remember that you are never
better than anyone else—you are simply better off.

—Great-Grandpa

$\mathcal{I}$t is not the failure of others to appreciate your abilities that
should trouble you, but rather your failure to appreciate theirs.

—Confucius

$\mathcal{I}$f your mental attitude changes constantly under
the pressure of tests, you are losing the battle of life.
He who is undefeated within is a truly victorious person.

—Paramhansa Yogananda

Be heroic.
—Dad

Sleep is one of the best meditations.
—the Dalai Lama

Ambition never comes to an end.
—Yoshida Kenko

By three methods we may learn wisdom: First, by reflection,
which is the noblest; second, by imitation, which is the easiest;
and third, by experience, which is the bitterest.
—Confucius

If you did not know your name, what name
would you give yourself?
—Dad

Ever climbing, ever reaching. Ever striving, ever surpassing.
Ever gaining, ever accumulating. For leaders these alone are the
ways to attain. And so for fifty years or more they repeat the pattern
until stopped by circumstances, by disillusion, or by death.

—Lao-tzu

Most people give in to their baser instincts, thinking more
of short-term pleasures and gains than the kind of sustained
self-restraint required to attain lasting success and happiness.

—Mahathir Mohamad

When you are selflessly generous with no concern for receiving
in kind, all you have given will return to you tenfold.

—Uncle Miller

When I despair, I remember that all through history
the way of truth and love has always won. There have been
tyrants and murderers and for a time they seem invincible
but in the end, they always fall . . . think of it—always.

—Mahatma Gandhi

Truth is indestructible, virtue is indestructible,
purity is indestructible.
—Vivekananda

Inner enlightenment leads naturally to outer enlightenment.
One man enlightening himself can help
countless others enlighten themselves.
—Dad

If you sacrifice your growth and talent for love, you will not find happiness. True happiness is obtained only by realizing your potential. Authentic love is a force that helps expand your life and achieve your potential with fresh and dynamic vitality.

—Daisaku Ikeda

Hope is the risk that must be run.

—Georges Bernanos

Sixty years ago, I knew everything; now I know nothing. Education is a progressive discovery of our own ignorance.

—Will Durant

Do not grow old, no matter how long you live. Never cease to stand like curious children before the Great Mystery into which we were born.

—Albert Einstein

Humor is falling down stairs when you
do it while warning your friend not to.
—Kenneth Bird

To be seventy years young is sometimes far more
cheerful and hopeful than to be thirty years old.
—Oliver Wendell Holmes

Never have I enjoyed being youthful
so thoroughly as I have in my old age.
—George Santayana

Your attraction to certain types of people
reveals less about your desire for those people and
more about your desire to become like those people.
—Dad

Luck is a dividend of sweat.
The more you sweat, the luckier you get.
—Ray Kroc

Go out on a limb. That's where the fruit is.
—Jimmy Carter

I take a simple view of living.
It is: keep your eyes open and get on with it.
—Laurence Olivier

Happiness is not an ideal of reason but of imagination.
—Immanuel Kant

There is no duty we so much underrate
as the duty of being happy.
—Robert Louis Stevenson

One's reaction to fortune often reveals more about one's character than one's reaction to misfortune.
—Dad

Character is power.
—Booker T. Washington

Do nothing which is of no value.
—Miyamoto Musashi

I don't believe in heaven or hell. They're here: you choose which one you're going to lodge in.
—Tony Parker

You can't separate peace from freedom because no one can be at peace unless he has his freedom.
—Malcolm X

One chance is all you need.
—Jesse Owens

Life is like a game of cards.
The hand you are dealt is destiny;
the way you play it is free will.
—Jawaharlal Nehru

The meeting of two personalities is like
the contact of two chemical substances;
if there is any reaction, both are transformed.
—Carl Jung

To act out the play of victory, you must decide that
you are going to win. Then visualize that result and engrave
it in your mind. When you manifest the doubtless
conviction that you can do it, then you can do it.
—Pascual Olivera

There are those who create and those who destroy—
always be a creator.

—Grandpa

Believe nothing, no matter where you read
it or who has said it, not even if I have said it,
unless it agrees with reason and common sense.

—Shakyamuni

You, in this very body, with this very mind, are worthy of all
the love and happiness in the world. If you can only awaken to
that truth, then all adversity will be transformed into joy.

—Daisaku Ikeda

Your worldly misdeeds may have piled up as high as the
tallest mountain, but when you chant *Nam-myoho-renge-kyo*
your evil karma will vanish like frost under the sun.

—Nichiren

*O*ne day
much too soon
the end will come
to each of our
precious brief lifetimes;
knowing this, live fearlessly;
leave unchallenged
not a single obstacle
between yourself
and the realization
of your most joyous dreams.
—Dad

父の道

BIOGRAPHICAL NOTES

Peter Abelard (1079–1144) French philosopher and theologian.

James Allen (1849–1925) U.S. novelist.

Aristotle (384–322 B.C.E.) Greek philosopher and legendary homosexual cultural figure; student of Plato at Academy in Athens; tutored Alexander the Great.

Saint Augustine (354–430) Known as Saint Augustine of Hippo; early Christian church father.

Benjamin Nnamdi Azikiwe (1904–1996) Nigerian statesman; first president of the Republic of Nigeria (1963–1966).

Richard Bach (1936–) U.S. author.

Francis Bacon (1561–1626) English philosopher and author.

Georges Bernanos (1888–1948) French novelist.

Josh Billings (1818–1885) Pseudonym of Henry Wheeler Shaw; U.S. humorist.

Kenneth Bird (1887–1965) British cartoonist under the pseudonym of Fougasse.

William Blake (1757–1827) English poet, painter, engraver, and mystic.

Ray Bradbury (1920–) U.S. novelist; works include *Fahrenheit 451*.

Sir Thomas Browne (1605–1682) English physician and author.

George Burns (1896–1996) U.S. vaudeville comedian and actor.

Lewis Carroll (1832–1898) Pseudonym of Charles Lutwidge Dodgson; English mathematician and writer; author of *Alice's Adventures in Wonderland* and *Through the Looking Glass*.

Jimmy Carter (1924–) Thirty-ninth U.S. president; received the Nobel Peace Prize (2002).

Lawrence Carter (1941–) First dean of Morehouse College's Martin Luther King Jr. International Chapel.

Cesar Chavez (1927–1993) U.S. labor leader; in 1962 founded the United Farm Workers.

Saint John Chrysostom (c. 347–407) Syrian prelate; archbishop of Constantinople.

Chuang-tzu (fourth century B.C.E.) Chinese philosopher and teacher.

Winston Churchill (1874–1965) British statesman and author; British prime minister from 1940 to 1945.

Cicero (106–43 B.C.E.) Roman orator, statesman, and philosopher.

Confucius (551–479 B.C.E.) Chinese philosopher and teacher.

James Fenimore Cooper (1789–1851) U.S. novelist.

Bill Cosby (1937–) U.S. comedian, writer, actor, and television producer.

Dad (1944–1989) Independent businessman, professional boxer, aviation safety specialist, and Taro Gold's father.

Dalai Lama (1935–) Spiritual and temporal head of Tibet, currently Tenzin Gyatso, designated the fourteenth Dalai Lama; received the Nobel Peace Prize in 1989.

Charles Darwin (1809–1882) English naturalist; outlined the theory of evolution.

Peter De Vries (1910–1993) U.S. novelist and short-story writer.

Charles Dickens (1812–1870) English novelist.

Diogenes (d. c. 320 B.C.E.) Greek philosopher.

John Dos Passos (1896–1970) U.S. novelist.

Fyodor Dostoyevsky (1821–1881) Russian novelist.

Will Durant (1885–1981) U.S. historian; won the Pulitzer Prize in 1967.

Albert Einstein (1879–1955) German-Swiss-American theoretical physicist; received the Nobel Prize in physics in 1921.

Ralph Waldo Emerson (1803–1882) U.S. essayist, philosopher, and poet.

Quintus Ennius (239–169 B.C.E.) Roman poet.

William Faulkner (1897–1962) U.S. novelist; received the Nobel Prize in literature in 1949.

B. C. Forbes (1880–1954) Scottish-born U.S. publisher; first publisher of *Forbes* magazine.

Malcolm Forbes (1919–1990) U.S. publisher; also editor and publisher of *Forbes* magazine.

Benjamin Franklin (1706–1790) U.S. statesman, diplomat, scientist, and inventor.

R. Buckminster Fuller (1895–1983) U.S. engineer and inventor.

Galileo Galilei (1564–1642) Italian mathematician, astronomer, and physicist.

Mahatma Gandhi (1869–1948) Mohandas K. Gandhi (Mahatma means "great soul"); Indian nationalist and spiritual leader; considered the father of independent India.

Kahlil Gibran (1883–1931) Lebanese author, poet, mystic, and artist.

Arthur Godfrey (1903–1983) U.S. radio personality and host.

Johann Wolfgang von Goethe (1749–1832) German poet and novelist.

Grandpa (1920–1999) Entrepreneur, writer, popular Southern California politician, and Taro Gold's grandfather.

Great-Grandpa (1895–1990) Banker, writer, and Taro Gold's great-grandfather.

Wayne Gretzky (1961–) Canadian ice hockey player.

Hafez (c. 1325–1389) Persian lyric poet.

Edward Frederick Halifax (1881–1954) British statesman.

Herbie Hancock (1940–) U.S. pianist, composer, and Nichiren Buddhist; received the Academy Award and multiple Grammy awards.

S. I. Hayakawa (1906–1992) Canadian-born U.S. semanticist, educator, and senator.

Don Herold (1889–1966) U.S. author and humorist.

Eric Hoffer (1902–1983) U.S. social writer.

Huang-po (b. Tang Dynasty) Chinese master of Chan Buddhism.

Victor Hugo (1802–1885) French writer.

Hubert Humphrey (1911–1978) U.S. politician; senator and vice president.

Aldous Huxley (1894–1963) English novelist and critic; grandson of T. H. Huxley.

T. H. Huxley (1825–1895) English biologist; grandfather of Aldous Huxley.

Henrik Ibsen (1828–1906) Norwegian poet and dramatist.

Daisaku Ikeda (1928–) President of the Soka Gakkai International Buddhist association; founder of the nonsectarian Soka School system and Soka University; received the United Nations Peace Award in 1983.

William James (1842–1910) U.S. psychologist and philosopher.

Thomas Jefferson (1743–1826) Third U.S. president; noted naturalist, scholar, and architect.

Jesus (c. 6 B.C.E.–c. 30 C.E.) Historical founder of Christianity, which grew out of his disciples' proclamation of his divinity.

Carl Jung (1875–1961) Swiss psychologist and psychiatrist; founder of analytic psychology.

Kalidasa (fifth century) Indian poet and dramatist; considered the greatest Indian writer.

Garrison Keillor (1942–) U.S. author, humorist, musician, and radio personality.

John Fitzgerald Kennedy (1917–1963) Thirty-fifth U.S. president; established the Peace Corps.

Martin Luther King, Jr. (1929–1968) U.S. clergyman, reformer, and civil rights leader; Baptist minister; advocate of nonviolence and racial brotherhood.

Rudyard Kipling (1865–1936) English poet and writer; began writing verse and tales in India and continued in England; received the Nobel Prize in literature in 1907.

Jiddu Krishnamurti (1895–1986) Indian who was prophesied to be the World Teacher of the Second Coming; well-known public speaker, educator, and author.

Ray Kroc (1902–1984) Founder of the McDonald's Corporation.

Akira Kurosawa (1910–1998) Japanese film director, producer, and screenwriter.

Kwan-tzu (d. 645 B.C.E.) Chinese politician and philosopher.

Lao-tzu (c. 604–531 B.C.E.) Chinese philosopher (name means "old master"); father of Taoism; his *Tao Te Ching* teaches detachment, going with the flow of nature.

Bruce Lee (1940–1973) U.S. actor, martial arts expert.

Leonardo da Vinci (1452–1519) Italian painter, sculptor, architect, engineer, and scientist.

Oscar Levant (1906–1972) U.S. pianist and composer.

Lin Yutang (1895–1976) Chinese author and philologist.

Abraham Lincoln (1809–1865) Sixteenth U.S. president; issued the Emancipation Proclamation, declaring freedom for all slaves.

Naguib Mahfouz (1911–) Egyptian novelist; received the Nobel Prize in literature in 1988.

Malcolm X (1925–1965) U.S. religious and social leader; converted to the Muslim faith while imprisoned for robbery (1946–1952) and later to orthodox Islam.

Nelson Mandela (1918–) South African lawyer and statesman; his country's first black president (1994–1999); received the Nobel Peace Prize in 1993.

Mao Zedong (1893–1976) Chinese soldier and statesman; became chairman of the People's Republic of China in 1949.

Marcus Aurelius (121–180) Roman emperor from 161 until his death.

Peter Marshall (1902–1949) Scottish-born American clergyman; chaplain to the U.S. Senate.

Konosuke Matsushita (1894–1989) Japanese industrialist.

Michelangelo (1475–1564) Italian sculptor, painter, architect, and poet.

Uncle Miller (1921–1991) Banker, community leader, and Taro Gold's great-uncle.

Miyamoto Musashi (1584–1645) Japanese soldier and artist.

Mahathir Mohamad (1925–) Former prime minister of Malaysia.

Michel de Montaigne (1533–1592) French Renaissance writer.

Thomas Moore (1779–1852) Irish poet.

Vladimir Nabokov (1899–1977) Russian-born U.S. writer whose works include *Lolita*.

Jawaharlal Nehru (1889–1964) Statesman and first prime minister of India (1947–1964); imprisoned several times by the British during the movement for an independent India.

Nichiren (1222–1282) Buddhist philosopher and religious reformer; established the practice of chanting *Nam-myoho-renge-kyo* to "polish one's inner mirror" of enlightenment.

Friedrich Nietzsche (1844–1900) German philosopher, poet, and writer.

Alfred Nobel (1833–1896) Swedish manufacturer, inventor, and philanthropist; invented dynamite in 1866; bequeathed funds to establish Nobel Prizes.

Okakura Kakuzo (1862–1913) Japanese art critic and author; cofounder of the Tokyo Fine Arts School and Japan Academy of Fine Arts.

Pascual Olivera (1944–2003) World-renowned flamenco dancer, choreographer, and inspiration for millions of fellow Nichiren Buddhists.

Laurence Olivier (1907–1989) English actor and director; starred in many notable films, including *Wuthering Heights* and *Hamlet*.

George Orwell (1903–1950) Pseudonym of Eric Arthur Blair; British author best known for his political satires, such as *1984* and *Animal Farm*.

Jesse Owens (1913–1980) U.S. athlete; Olympic gold medalist and civic leader; participated in the 1936 summer Olympics in Berlin in front of Adolf Hitler.

Thomas Paine (1737–1809) U.S. political philosopher and author; published *Common Sense* during the American Revolution in 1776.

Norman Vincent Peale (1898–1993) U.S. religious leader and writer.

Christopher Reeve (1952–2004) U.S. film and stage actor; his efforts to recover from paralysis and to support handicapped children and paraplegics brought worldwide admiration.

Franklin D. Roosevelt (1882–1945) Thirty-second U.S. president; held office an unprecedented four terms through the Great Depression and World War II.

Theodore Roosevelt (1858–1919) Twenty-sixth president of the United States; received the Nobel Peace Prize in 1906.

Bertrand Russell (1872–1970) English mathematician and philosopher; received the Nobel Prize in literature in 1950.

Oscar Arias Sánchez (1941–) Costa Rican politician and author; president of Costa Rica (1986–1990); received the Nobel Peace Prize in 1987.

George Santayana (1863–1952) Spanish-born U.S. poet and philosopher.

Friedrich von Schiller (1759–1805) German poet, playwright, and critic.

Charles M. Schulz (1922–2000) U.S. cartoonist, creator of the comic strip *Peanuts* (starting in 1950).

Chief Seattle (1786?–1866) American Suquamish Indian chief; the city of Seattle is named after him.

Seneca (c. 4 B.C.E.–65 C.E.) Called Seneca the Younger; Roman statesman and philosopher.

William Shakespeare (1564–1616) English dramatist and poet.

Shakyamuni (c. 563–c. 483) Born a prince of the Shakya clan; renounced his royal status to begin a religious quest; his teachings are the foundation of Buddhism.

Shantiveda (eighth century) Indian philosopher and writer.

George Bernard Shaw (1856–1950) British playwright and critic; received the Nobel Prize in literature in 1925.

Sima Qian (145–90 B.C.E.) Also known as Ssu-ma Ch'ien; Chinese historian, astronomer.

Sri Swami Sivananda (1887–1963) Indian Hindu religious leader.

Sophocles (c. 496–405 B.C.E.) Athenian playwright and legendary homosexual cultural figure who wrote into his nineties; most famous for *Oedipus Tyrannus*.

John Steinbeck (1902–1968) U.S. novelist; in 1939 won the Pulitzer Prize for *The Grapes of Wrath* and in 1962 received the Nobel Prize in literature.

Robert Louis Stevenson (1850–1894) Scottish essayist, novelist, and poet.

Sun-tzu (fourth century B.C.E.) Chinese writer; reputed author of *The Art of War*; his insistence on political aspects of war influenced modern strategists.

Charles Swindoll (1934–) U.S. religious writer and educator.

Tecumseh (1768–1813) American Shawnee Indian chief.

Danny Thomas (1914–1991) U.S. actor, well known for his starring role in *Make Room for Daddy* (1953–1964); founded St. Jude Children's Research Hospital in 1962.

Henry David Thoreau (1817–1862) U.S. essayist and poet; associated with the Transcendentalist movement.

Josei Toda (1900–1958) Founder of the Soka Gakkai (Value-Creating Society) with his mentor, Tsunesaburo Makiguchi; met with persecution, including imprisonment, during World War II for his commitment to human rights.

J. R. R. Tolkien (1892–1973) British writer; works include the Lord of the Rings trilogy.

Leo Tolstoy (1828–1910) Russian novelist and moral philosopher.

Arnold Toynbee (1889–1975) English historian.

Mark Twain (1835–1910) Pseudonym of Samuel L. Clemens; U.S. writer.

Henry Van Dyke (1852–1933) U.S. clergyman and writer.

Vivekananda (1863–1902) Indian religious leader.

Voltaire (1694–1778) pseudonym of François-Marie Arouet; French philosopher and writer.

Lech Walesa (1943–) Polish trade unionist; received the Nobel Peace Prize in 1983; president of the Republic of Poland, the country's first post-Communist leader (1990–1995).

Booker T. Washington (1856–1915) U.S. educator and author; born a slave; in 1881 appointed to establish and head Tuskegee Institute.

Walt Whitman (1819–1892) U.S. poet and legendary homosexual cultural figure; publications include *Leaves of Grass*.

Elie Wiesel (1928–2005) Romanian-born U.S. writer; Holocaust survivor; devoted his adult life to writing and speaking about the Holocaust; received the Nobel Peace Prize in 1986.

Oscar Wilde (1854–1900) Irish playwright, poet, and legendary homosexual cultural figure.

Wu Ting-fang A contemporary of Sun Yat-sen; served as foreign minister and a diplomat in Washington, D.C.

Paramhansa Yogananda (1893–1952) Indian yogi and guru; founded the Self-Realization Fellowship headquartered in Southern California in 1920.

Yoshida Kenko (1283–1350) Japanese poet and essayist.

Muhammad Yunus (1940–) Bangladeshi banker; in 1976 founded the Grameen Bank, with branches around the world, which focuses on making loans to the poor based on principles of trust and solidarity.

GLOWCHILD

And other Poems

GLOWCHILD

And other Poems
Selected and with introduction

by RUBY DEE

ODARKAI BOOKS

THE THIRD PRESS

JOSEPH OKPAKU PUBLISHING CO., INC.
444 CENTRAL PARK WEST,
NEW YORK, N.Y. 10025

Library of Congress Catalogue Card Number: LC 72-77858

SBN 89388-040-X

PRINTED IN THE U.S.A.

Designed by BENNIE ARRINGTON

ODARKAI BOOKS,
named after the mother of the publisher
of The Third Press, is the Juvenile
and Children's book imprint of The Third Press.

First Printing October, 1972

Acknowledgements

I wish to express my gratitude to the students and former students of Albert Leonard Junior High School and New Rochelle High School whose poems form the basis of this anthology.

My sincere thanks go to Ellen Brickers and Lorna Sloan who typed and checked the manuscript; to Ann Williams who put us in touch with teachers and students; to my children Nora, Guy and LaVerne who tapped their own minds and those of their friends; to my husband Ossie, who encouraged me to finish the project.

R. D.

The publishers wish to acknowledge their gratitude for permission to publish the following poems:

"Less Majeste" from *Rhymes For the Irreverent* by E.Y. Harburg. © 1965 Reprinted by permission of Grossman Publishers.

"Glow Child" by Constance E. Berkley, from *Freedomways Magazine* Vol 7, No 2, 1967. Reprinted by permission of *Freedomways Magazine.*

"Today Is Ours Let's Live It" from *Freedomways Magazine* Vol 4, No 1, 1964. Author unknown. Reprinted by permission of *Freedomways Magazine.*

"Birth" by Linda Thomas, from *Freedomways Magazine* Vol 8, No 1, 1968. Reprinted by permission of *Freedomways Magazine.*

"When" by Rakeman (Mathura Mustapha). © May 1971 by *Black World*. Reprinted by permission of *Black World* and the author.

"The Beat" by James R. Lucas. © September 1968 by Negro Digest. Reprinted by permission of *Black World* and the author.

"Me And Santa" by Robert T. Bowen, from *Liberator*, Vol 9, No 12, 1960. Reprinted by permission of *Liberator.*

"First Paradox" and "A Welfare Mother" by Glenn Hines, from *Liberator* Vol 10, No 4, 1970. Reprinted by permission of *Liberator.*

"Michigan Autumn" by Othello Mahome, from *Liberator* Vol 10, No 12, 1970. Reprinted by permission of *Liberator.*

"Peace" (excerpt) by Paul Eluard, from *Thou Shalt Not Overkill*, © 1969 by Walter Lowenfels. Reprinted by permission of Walter Lowenfels.

"A Song of Peace," from *Thou Shalt Not Overkill* ©1969 by Walter Lowenfels and reprinted with his permission.

"There's A Raindrop," by Lisa McCann, from *Liberation* Vol XIII, No 8, 1969. Reprinted by permission of *Liberation.*

"Watch Your English," author unknown, from MACA Adoption Newsletter, Fall 1969. Reprinted by permission of the Chairman.

I dedicate these poems to the next-time people, to the hearts and minds and souls and determinations of the now children who will inherit the pieces.

Ruby Dee

CONTENTS

INSIDE, OUTSIDE BLACK

BY THE WAY POLITICAL

CITY HAPPENINGS

INTRODUCTION

Whenever I have been called upon to read poetry to Junior High School people, I have felt a bit uncomfortable. It is easier to find material for adults or for younger children. My notebook contained so few selections that seemed to make a real impression; and I had read them so often. I had however, already begun to increase my repertoire to teenagers when John Henrik Clarke, the Editor of *Freedomways*, suggested me for an assignment on just such a collection—poetry geared to the "between cycle" group—the younger teenagers from about eleven to around seventeen.

I am not sure I know how to judge the literary value of a poem. I know little about meter and style and form; but I do know when I am affected, where an idea grabs me and makes me want to laugh or cry or just sit and think a while. I have listened to the poems that youngsters themselves have chosen to read for various school programs and noted their reactions as an audience when something especially meaningful is presented. Most important for now, however, is the fact that I have included in this book some of the thoughts gathered from what they have written themselves.

Sometimes I have found a poem that feels young—because it answers some of the questions I have listened to or expresses, with candor and simplicity, concerns common to us all. These poets describe what is known but not said, what is felt but seldom cried out, or what is too ridiculous to respect. These gifted people write frankly—often with heartbreak, often with hope—about what they feel. They say "How I hate, How I love." Yes, and they complain and feel the grief of life. There is a yearning to increase and deepen their knowledge sooner, and faster. Fourteen- and sixteen-year-olds questioning the nature of existence itself and searching for personal definition, I find a challenging common denominator of our lives. For example, Linda Thomas in her poem "Birth," asks "why am I here"? and then describes the kind of world in which she wants to be born.

There are descriptions of poverty and discrimination and poems of self-criticism and of judgment of peers. Most stimulating for me are the poems dealing with abstractions. Time, Unity, Soul, Love, Peace, Freedom—themes so often taken for granted—beg for a more precise definition in the minds of these young people.

I have also experienced, in my sessions with a young audience, enthusiastic response to poems of encouragement and affirmation based on reality and truth. "Today is Ours" is a favorite.

What would a collection like this be without some nonsense, a riddle or two, and a chance to laugh? I have therefore included some humorous poems such as "Santa And Me," where fun is intermingled with fact.

I have also included a few items of advice from oldsters to youngsters because they were reasonably well tolerated and because I want to sound like a parent from time to time. A mutual delight in this category is "The Spider and Fly Thing"—a neat and humorous tale of parental disobedience. I wanted to come up with a book that, besides stating some of the hard facts of our time, would encourage the reader to think about solutions where beauty and freedom and fun and truth and love may become finally the main event. I have mostly entertained urban children who live in disadvantaged communities, and so I gathered this material especially with them in mind. I believe the poor child, whether Indian, black, Puerto Rican or white, often thinks of himself as being outside the good life, alone in a grey kind of misery. That is the way it has been presented to him all too often. Sometimes he believes it. Sometimes he tries to prove it.

Poetry, which is also music of the soul, can help point the way to a more positive connection to life. Poets help us to become a group. The group then, through its songs, its legends, its battles, becomes a shelter—a cocoon—from which its young people can emerge better prepared to help advance the group, and with a clearer understanding of personal responsibility. Also, there is a comfort in knowing that one belongs to a group, and to a continuing line of experience. The job of young people becomes, therefore, to catch up quickly on the past, while dealing with the present, in order to focus faster on the goals of a better world; on the goals of a better people in that better world that must surely come. To set the next stage, I believe poetry helps.

I have collected this volume of poetry from the young and not so young, mixed them together and tried to make a book that growing minds would want to read, would want to learn a poem or two from. It is my hope, finally, that after reading this they will be encouraged to add to the written treasury.

NATURE, LOVE, PASSION, FUN

I LOVE. . .

I love, the birds that sing to me in the
Birth of morning.

I love, the cold clear water on my skin to wake
My rested face.

I love, walking briskly through the clean
Crisp noon air.

I love, to see people being
People together.

I love, to see love being loved
Don't you?

LaVerne Davis
New Rochelle H.S.

"ESCAPE"

Have you ever watched a fly trying to get out a
        window?
It yearns for the sunshine on its back, and lost freedom.
It goes back and forth trying to get out.
Maybe it's trying to tell US something.
Should WE also try to get out,
Get back to the outdoors,
Escape from the prison called civilization?
To where a man is free and doesn't die from 9 – 5.
Where he's not boxed in by responsibility.
Yes, maybe WE also should be looking for the
space in the window to Escape.

Robert Kaufmann
Albert Leonard Jr. H.S.

TODAY IS A KILLER

I often sit and stare at the sea
   and dream dreams
     and hope hopes
       and wish wishes

And lately
   I listen to the wind song
   as it dances a beautiful dance for me
   but these moments
       these moments never
         never seem to last too long
        for after the hopes
            dreams

                and wishes

and after singing
   dancing wind
after you and me and a stolen moment of happiness
   after a glimpse at the
     timeless
       natural universe
     moving in effortless beauty
   comes the stark reality of today
today
     grinning his fiendish

all-knowing grin

                    today

his ugly face pressed firmly against mine

                    today

staring at me with lifeless eyes

                    today

washing away all memories of

        yesterday's dreams,

    crumbling hopes

        destroying wishes . . .

    today
      today
        today
          today   is a killer

David Nelson

LA VIE

A little wave came and kissed my legs
and rippled on away.
A middle-sized wave washed in on me
and seemed inclined to stay.
Another wave, puppy-playful, came
and slapped me in the chest
and knocked me down — and silly me,
I liked that one the best.

Alfred Duckett

WITH RISING PASSIONS

With rising passions
    our feelings grew.
Suddenly, merely holding you
    could not satisfy me.
With the warmth of your breasts
    generating anxiety
    within my heart,
I lost consciousness
    establishing you as
    the representation of my innerself.
I then sought to join
    my innerself.
With pounding urgency
    our hearts played
    in harmony.
Then stripping ourselves
    of all barriers
We made love. . .
    moving to such a beat
    that we played a hostile tune.
We fought. . .
    as we loved. . .
And baby
    we won. . .

Calvin Anderson
New Rochelle H.S.

ISN'T LIFE PECULIAR?

"Isn't life peculiar?" said Jeremy.
"Compared to what?" replied the spider.

Author Unknown

THE OPTIMIST

The optimist fell ten stories.
At each window bar
He shouted to his friends:
"All right so far."

Author Unknown

THERE'S A RAINDROP

There's a raindrop starin' in the window
Wonder what it wants maybe it's bored
and wants some company well so do i
want to go out get soaking wet feel the rain
then come back and tell everyone
about it bet it can't be as bad as sittin alone
in the broadway central knowing you love
and not knowing quite what to do about it
and all these words can't really express
they only give you an idea
'bout what's really happening
inside my mind and it's restless
and i want to go out and do things
cause i am young and i love and i feel
and why shouldn't i go out
and live or at least catch
some strange tropical disease
instead of a lousy cold.

Lisa McCann

MEDITATION

I find you
behind the warm/cool darkness
of eyes closed

Afire, yes
The single flame within
guiding the way without

You are the words of all my scriptures
. . . my verses
. . . my songs

I find you waiting
Deep down
Beneath my truest silence

My entirety at rest,
I sit transfixed,
Spellbound by your nearness

You are motion stilled.

I find you in all corners of being
I become the child, and you the father/mother
of all happiness.

You are mine,
Ours,
And always the Saviour,
. . . Peace.

Nora Davis

ME AND SANTA

Santa Claus
I hate you because
You stink.
You and your one night stand
You and your grubby hand

Your toys, and joys, and silly poise
You funky bastard
You take more than you could ever give
'Cause you've got nothing to give and
    still you want to live
In the hearts of those whose parts
You soon will scatter in the streets

Santa Claus
I hope you get stuck
    in a slum chimney
I hope your bomb-totin' sleigh
Backfires and smoke-stains
    your jolly bottom
You've got an unrighteous nerve
    to laugh or even smile,
You skunk. You ought to
Walk
    from house to house and
    get down on your fat knees
    and beg,
"Please forgive me for I
know not what I do."

You aren't holy
You aren't special
You are a jinx, a hoax
To fool the folks.

Go some place — far away
Skat, cat
You rotten-ize an already
Sick humanity
Go get yourself last hired and
    quickly fired in a hell
    reddened by your own tattered suit.

You foggy freak of a madman —
Sit on your own western lap
    and pee on yourself,
Go hungry a few times and
    then choke yourself with Christmas
    candy: bright and sticky.
Go cold one night and
    then
Cover yourself with eight reindeer.

You know what you stand for:
You stand for yourself.
You're a holiday pimp.
Stuffed with zeroes and dollars.
And fearful hollers
    you can't and don't
    bring comfort. You bring
    constipation
You are envy
You are jealousy
You are pettiness and noise
    and emptiness

By January you've forgotten your
Own name
Where are you then, Oh Bloated One?
Counting receipts?
Patrolling the streets?
    or
Smiling from your cheats

to be
Improved upon next year?

You bring grief, you Bearded Grab Bag
And you don't give a shit about children.
And I'm gonna help them learn about
You
    and your sleigh — full of bad habits
I'm through with you and you know it
I hate you and now you know that, too.

May your snow melt
    and
In the chilly waters that follow
May you DROWN!!

Robert T. Bowen

FIRST OF THE YEAR LETTER

I did not send out Christmas cards this year
with fat, white Santa Clauses or white snow.
I did not hang the holly, did not dress a tree.
For it has occurred to me
that Christmases of days gone by
no longer need to be.

I did not search for Christmas cards
with Santas tinted black or brown
or satin maids with Afro haids
sent into the ghetto to enrich the folks downtown.

I did not send out Christmas cards
to advertise my trade.
Or to advertise my love
for the few, true friends I've made.

I gave a party for a child
and other children came.
I visited a friend in jail
with a number and no name.

I sat in meditation and came to realize
that part of being truly black
is refusing to tell white lies.

And so I think of things that are
and things that should not be.
And the Christmases of days gone by
are nevermore for me.

The biggest white lie is "peace on earth,"
For peace on earth is not.
And another is goodwill toward men
which mainly is forgot.
And as long as there are hungry babes,
And as long as there is war,
I mean to find some other paths
than I have trod before.

I mean to find some ways to make
Christmas become more true.
And neighbor, I would like to ask
what do you intend to do?

Alfred Duckett

THE SPIDER AND FLY THING

"Come into my parlor," said the spider to the fly.
"Come on, dig m' little pad — let's, you and I, get high!"
"Mr. Spider," said Miss Fly, "For me you may have eyes
But my mother always told me spiders eat up flies."
Said the spider to the fly, "Don't listen t' y' ma!
I wouldn't eat you, little fly. Y' know that-ha-ha-ha."
He spoke so convincingly, she ventured to his lair,
'Twasn't long before Miss Fly had cobwebs in her hair.
Mr. Spider he was hip and he romanced Miss Fly;
Did just what he promised and served what gets flies high.
Brought out favorite "looseners" meant to send them to the
   sky
And pretty soon, there in his web, he had a high little
   fly.
Ol' Spider lay back coolin', that smile of his was wry;
Miss Fly was gigglin'. Spider thought "Hm-dig this fly
   li'l' fly!"

That fly lived longer in a web than any fly I know
Cause when a fly flies in a web, that fly is booked to go!
Ol' Spider was a lover, he sure knew how to play;
He loosed Miss Fly. "Of course," he mused, "She'll come
   back one fine day."

She did too — oh yes she did — as soon as soon could be
She told her mama, "Girl, Mr. Spider b'longs t' me!
Idea tellin' me," she buzzed, "that spiders eat up flies.
I don't dig you, Mama — just plain unhip, I surmise."
Told ol' Spider all she said and how her ma had cried,
Said she wasn't sorry that her parent she'd defied.

Spider hung back in his web and everything was great,
Then — "Alright, Little Fly, come on! 'T's gettin' kind o'
   late."

In his eyes she saw that glint, her heart began to heave
And then it came to her. "Oh, Mr. Spider, I must leave!"
"Aw come on, girl! Now what's your story, what you gonna
do?
You're in my web, you're mine now, Honey — I've got news
f' you!
Miss Fly got thinking 'bout her ma, the things her ma had
said;
She'd disobeyed the old fly, now she's 'bout t' lose her
head.
'If I had only listened t' the mother I adore
But I was such an insect — like those humans more 'n' more!
I hope that other little flies will hear about my plight
'N' when their mothers warn them, they'll obey with all
their might."
"Hm," ol' Spider gloated, "Yes, Miss Fly, you are my
cup,"
With that he fell upon her — yow — and gobbled Miss Fly up.

Lesson: To all little flies
         And others who may think they're wise:—
         Fly flew by and Spider spied her.
         Miss Fly's mama tried to guide her
         But Miss Fly up, and defied her,
         Found herself—in Mr. Spider.

Emett "Babe" Wallace

THOUGHT I WAS GONNA DIE

I was walking, now I'm talking
Telling you what happened
I got up from Bed
& hit my head
Thought I was gonna diiie

Walked & tried to find the light
& found it allright
except now it's in my arm
Thought I was gonna diiiiiiiiie

Walked into the wall
instead of the Hall
turned around
like a ship aground
Thought I was gonna diiiiiiiiiiiiie

My sister then yelled
you woke me up you —
Went downstairs
Feeling like rotten pears
Thought I was gonna diiiiiiiiiiiiie

I kept knowing
I'v got to keep going
To get that thing I wanted
missed a step
went down in a Rush
Thought I was gonna diiiiiiiiiiiie

Walked to the door
but it wasn't there
& I thought it isn't Fair
Finally found it & looked outside
The paper wasn't even theeeeeere.

Billy Sipser
Albert Leonard Jr. H.S.

WATCH YOUR ENGLISH

We'll begin with a box, and the plural is boxes;
But the plural of ox is oxen, not oxes.
Then one fowl is a goose, but two are called geese,
Yet the plural of moose should never be meese!
You may find a lone mouse or a whole nest of mice,
But the plural of house is houses, not hice!
If the plural of man is always called men,
Why shouldn't the plural of pan be called pen?
If I speak of a foot, and you show me your feet,
And I give you a boot — would a pair be called beet?
If one is a tooth, and a whole set are teeth,
Why should not the plural of booth be called beeth?
Then one may be that and three would be those,
Yet hat in the plural would never be hose;
And the plural of cat is cats, not cose!
We speak of a brother, and also of brethren,
But though we say mother, we never say methren!
Then the masculine pronouns are he, his and him,
But imagine the feminine, she, shis and shim!
So English, I fancy, you all will agree
Is the funniest language you ever did see!

Author Unknown

RETORT

And Liz got mad and said:
"Man, you ain't shit!"

And I said: "No, I ain't.
But Liz,
You is."

Ruth Duckett Gibbs

20

A LOVE POEM

Tranquil is my inner self
externally my serious appearance remains
internally my heart smiles broadly
the smell of your perfume still remains
within my system,
as it fills each thirsty molecule I feel my
body relaxing, much in the same way I did
while in your arms.
feeling as though we were merely spirits of a pure
love existing no where and slowly drifting in a
mist of your sweet perfume.
Naked and pure we drift on through clouds
rich in color and in fragrance
infatuated with this halcyon existence
I reach for you.
as we float closer and closer towards
each other I open my arms to
receive you
I can see you floating into them; I close my arms
to embrace you
but I feel nothing.
Now suddenly I feel your eyes in the back of my head
your Breasts Bulging from my Back
your heart parallel to mine
your thighs in my legs
and then
I realize
I can never embrace you
for we are
one. . .

Calvin Anderson

THOUGHTS AND QUESTIONS ABOUT "ME"

LOOKING AT A LITTLE BABY

Looking at a little baby
All crinkly and small
Screaming with its miniature lungs making itself known
to the world
Young
So much life,
Makes me realize
how twisted my body in all kinds of knots
Adjusting and readjusting
Compromise
Overeating
out of anger,
Overdrinking
out of self pity.
Stretching
myself out of proportion.
What a fool I've been.

Gordon Nelson

I'M A VERY MIXED UP PERSON

I'm a very mixed up person
Playing very mixed up games
My mind feels like a complex
Machine and it's usually
Out of order.

Susan Robbins
Albert Leonard Jr. H.S.

DEAD LETTER

Dear You,

Why don't you be somebody
    that I can love?

     (signed)

     Me

Dear Who,

    Why don't you be
      somebody?

Frank S. Jenkins

MY FRIEND

MY FRIEND —
He is the most fabulous person —
    everything I've always
        wanted
           to be.

He is generous and Kind —
    forgiving and thoughtful —
        full of love and laughter.
        MY FRIEND —
           is ME.

Beth Hollender
Albert Leonard Jr. H.S.

I USED TO BE JAILED

I used to be jailed
    but now I am free,
It used to be I,
    but now it is we,
When I was enclosed
    I thought I was free,
But now that I'm open
    I know that I'm me
Just one part of we.

Jim Estrin
Albert Leonard Jr. H.S.

"MAMA, I DON'T KNOW"

When I was young, my mama used to ask me,
    "Boy, where are you goin' to live?"
And I said,
    "Mama I don't know."
And she would talk to me, and tell me not to
    make the mistakes of my papa.
And she said,
    "Boy, where are you goin' to work?"
And I said,
    "Mama, I don't know."
She would tell me how she lived in the streets,
    sleeping, and eating there.
And she said,
    "Boy what are you goin' to do?"
And I said,
    "Mama, I don't know."
And she put her head on my lap,
And she cried.

Pam Brown
Albert Leonard Jr. H.S.

I'VE YEARNED TO BECOME

I've yearned to become
invisible, to stop living
cast forever out of life

I've been lost in the fog of
fear . . .
My body seeming to be afire
afraid to sleep
afraid to scream or ask for help
then . . .
there was a delight I had
caught by seeing the sun
fading into the stretching
horizon.

the moon was climbing up the sky
then showed great pleasantness all around me
I had been kissed cooly of sensuality
when the dew came on my cheeks and shins
as I ran along the rocks by the water

I was happy to be alive
for those few hours

Daryl Branche

THE LIGHT THAT CONSTANTLY SHINES

The light that constantly shines above
Designs to turn me into a child of love
But I am a shadow and I cannot see
I believe it's the hardships of days gone by
That hide that light from me.

Gordon Nelson

... NOTHING ...

... Nothing.
Still you say nothing.
He asks to see you after class.
You nod your head in assent, so as not to let him
Notice the lump in your throat.

You stay after class. He says
"Jim, is there anything wrong?" You say no.

You are ashamed, for it is the
first time you intentionally lied to Mr. Foster.
He says "I'm sorry Jim, but
I can't pass you."

You walk the two miles home,
even though you have twenty cents for the bus.
You feel sick, ashamed, and guilty.
You know now that you hate
Mr. Foster's guts. You think of every four letter
foul word that you can call him, but refrain from
saying them out loud, lest someone hear you.

You reach your large home. You
pass up the chance to admire the fresh paint on
the picket fence, the new grass coming up.

Mother greets you with a message at
the door, but you grunt in reply, thus cutting off
any conversation between the two of you, for she
sees you don't want to talk.
You go up to your room, the largest
one of all the children's bedrooms.
You carefully lock the door. You
go to the bed and lie down.

Efrein Matos
Albert Leonard Jr. H.S.

You Cry.

BIRTH

Born of the sperm of the father
And the seed of the mother
Born in a world of love
And a world of hate
Born in a world of truth
And a world of lies.
Born into the world of the prejudiced
And into the world of the unbiased.

Eyes open to a glaring light
And the touch of strange hands
Eyes open to strange faces
And an unfamiliar environment
Eyes open and close
And become moist with tears

Ears open to sound which has no meaning
And sounds which are harsh
Ears open to its own sound
And it does not understand
Ears open to gun fire
And to screams
Ears open to cursing
And shouting

Mouth opens to utter the
Cries of revolt
And of distress
Mouth opens in surprise
AND ASKS, WHY? WHY AM I HERE?
Mouth opens in wonder
AND SAYS NO, NOT NOW, THE TIME IS WRONG
I want to be born in a world only of love
I want to be born in a world only of truth
I want to be born in a world only of the unbiased
I want to be born in a world only of peacefulness
And I want to be born in a world only of soft and
Wondrous words.

Linda Thomas

NIGHTMARE

I needed to think me a thought one day.
But a thought just wouldn't come.
So I opened my skull
Went inside my head
To see what the stoppage was from.
Snakes, rats, bats, maggots
Hyenas spiders and cats
Were doing stumptoe
In the wrinkles of my brain.
I said scat, go
You stinking creatures
This ain't a balcony
For your double features.
I puked and I cried as I
Snapped my skull back
The nerve of those varmints
Without paying rent
To move in and
Mess up my mind
I was going to think me a
Righteous thought
But with all that dead shit
Between my ears
Sweet Jesus, I just can't.

But I showed em'
I fixed em
I got me a head transplant.

Anonymous

I WISH

I wish everyone could have
Their own field
With flowers,
To run and play and do just anything in;
Anytime,
To be alone,
And Free —
Free from tension worry and trouble;
To think,
And sometimes,
You could bring your dog and your friends
And just talk,
Or play —
Roll around in the grass, do headstands, somersaults,
Let your body relax and do anything it wants.
The birds, worms, and the snakes and the caterpillers
Would be there
As your friends.
You would communicate with them;
Not talk — communicate!
And . . .
Understand nature, your field, animals, and yourself.

Risa Gerson
Albert Leonard, Jr. H.S.

I WANT

I want calm without the whisky
I want peace without the pills
I want love without an exchange rate
To give a gift unstrained.
I want to want less of what I see
To give up much of what I've got
I want to be thankful
I want to know joy, pure and free of guilt.
I want to care for others in spirit and in truth
I want to know God's reason for my life
I want the strength to suffer and conquer evil
I want that which is good to be strong, fulfilling
To feel my oneness with the source of life
I want omniscience, omnipresence & omnipotence
To give me a kiss.

Ann Wallace

I KNOW WHAT THE SOUL IS

I know what the soul is —
It's a little man inside you
That keeps on hollering
"Let me out!"
"Let Me out!"

Guy Davis

I AM NOWHERE

I am nowhere
With thousands of people
About me.

I am imprisoned
With my ebony skin
Allowed to converse with a few
Who do not fear their peers.

Allowed to be a human being
Behind closed doors.
And it's secondary citizen
In public.

I feel my people's loneliness now
More than ever
I feel a need for my fellow man.
For I am his peer
No more.
And damned sure
No less.

Calvin Anderson
New Rochelle H.S.

INSIDE, OUTSIDE BLACK

SCIENCE . . .

Science
   tells you
      Black is the
         absence of light

but
   your soul
      tells you Black
         is the light of the
           world.

Gordon Nelson

COLORS

Colors of Animals
Colors of Trees, Sky, Water
Colors of Cars and Clothes
How Fine
Colors of Fruit
No Dispute
Colors of Wine
Colors of Flowers and Jewels
How Divine
What are We
Rapping Over
Scrapping Over
Frying Over
Dying Over
Colors of People
How Assinine!

Ruth Duckett Gibbs

TO WHOM IT DOES CONCERN
BLUE IS MY FAVORITE COLOR

Blue is my favorite color,
    but all I see is red.
As I look at your eyes I see red,
    reflecting the broken blood vessels in
    my tear drawn eyes.
As I look at your lips I touch red,
    reenacting the passion which once lay
    between your lips and mine.
As I look at your arms I feel red,
    remembering the long embraces
    we once held.
As I look in your soul I sense red,
    realising you are no longer special
    or tender caring.
As I look in your mind I find red,
    imbedded in disrespect for black women
    and their needs as black people.
As I look in your heart I am red
    with the hungry vibrations
    of revenge.
Blue is my favorite color, but all I see is red.

La Verne Davis

WHAT'S IN A WORD?

Perhaps, when Shakespeare lived
A rose
By any other term might smell as sweet.
But now, Man,
what's in a word is out of sight.
What's in a word
Can make you switch or fight.
Negro! Nigger! Black! White!
What's in a word?
The IMAGE, Man!
What's in a word?
Dynamite!

Ruth Duckett Gibbs

UNDERNEATH THE BLACK POET-TREE

Black Poetry is not
what Shakespeare begot.
Nor is it one
with Tennyson.
It's psychedelic beats
have little in common
with Shelley and Keats.
It has its own diameter.
Not iambic pentameter.
It has upon it
no rule of sonnet.
No straight-laced corset.
Nothing to force it.
It shrieks. It streaks.
It belts. It melts.
It sings. It swings.
It cries. It laughs
in verses or in paragraphs.
It grooves. It moves.
It's canny - Giovanni.
It clues — Langston Hughes.
It cooks — Gwen Brooks.
It's a dream's godson.
Dig Owen Dodson.
It makes you see.
Hip to Don Lee?
It has undertones
Like LeRoi Jones.
It's a brand new school.
Both hot and cool.
A blues beat.
Bittersweet.
It's a deep, deep blue.

Bright red, high yellow.
It's loud.
It's proud.
It's a wilder strum.
A super-drum.
It sets up its own condition.
Defies tradition.
It shocks. It rocks.
It mocks. It knocks.
It's humor. Drama.
It talks about your mama.
It's love. It's dissension.
It's a brand new dimension.
It's many, many track.
So come, sit down with me
and spiel and spat and
soul-rap and spree
beneath this looming,
blooming,
black —
black poet-tree.

Alfred Duckett
Ruth Duckett Gibbs

GLOWCHILD

Black child . . . so small
   Tiny segment of wondrous color
Who would ever think
   That you
Who are so unsung in song
   Could all at once shimmer
   Like a heavy sun
Turning night-time to day
   In one small face
When laughter peels from your throat
   Pulling back the full lips
Sending sunrays through the field of your face
   And the white gleam of your teeth
Highlights the dark contours of your cheeks . . .

Constance E. Berkley

IT WASN'T JUST THE RAIN

When I was just a little girl,
    about 8 or 9 years old,

We moved to a new neighborhood,
    our old house we sold.

I dressed and went outside to play,
    but no one was around.

I guess since it was rainy out,
    they did not like wet ground.

The next day it was beautiful,
    I went outside again.

But still no one was out to play,
    it wasn't just the rain.

I saw faces through the windows,
    big eyes wide and glaring.

I knew they were the children,
    I knew why they were staring.

It wasn't the rain that kept them in,
    it wasn't the rain at all.

It was the color of my skin,
    a "Nigger" as they call.

Pam Brown
Albert Leonard Jr. H.S.

365 DAYS OF WINTER

365 Days of Winter!
I woke up one Black morning, in one
of my Black moods.
Feeling good —
Well I put on my Black clothes,
went into my Black bathroom, and combed
my natural kinky Black hair.
Went into my Black kitchen and fixed
myself a Black soul meal.
Then I went to my Black closet, put on
my Black coat,
Picked up my Black boots,
Walked down my Black stairs,
Opened up my Black door . . .
I bet you can't guess what my Black eyes
saw . . .
. . . White Snow!!

Joyce Milton
Albert Leonard Jr. H.S.

I SEEM TO BE/BUT NOW I AM

I seem to be Evil, Mean, Ugly
  Maybe I am

They say I am full of Hate.
  I can Be that too

  I feel that all
I have to do is stay
  Black and Die.

Rhonda Metz
Albert Leonard Jr. H.S.

SET DOWN, GAL

Little black woman!
You my queen.
I'm gonna buy you
another scene.

Gonna set you down
from fighting for me.
Huh! You think Lincoln
set you free?

Gonna buy you everything
a man's wife should have
when he's a king.

Set down, gal!

I don't mean wigs
or Cadillacs.
I don't mean the Quality
of Saks.

I don't mean What Mrs. Whitey has
or what she do.
I mean I'm gonna buy you
your own black you!!

Set down, gal!
Set down, sweet, black gal!
Set!

Alfred Duckett

IF EVERYONE ELSE IS WALKING

If everyone else is walking
    and you own a car. What does that make you?

If everyone is starving
    and you got a good job. What does that make you?

If everyone else is cold
    and you got a warm big house. What does that make
       you?

If everyone else is dead
    and you are alive with blackness. What does that
       make you?

    ALONE!

Gordon Nelson

BEAUTIFUL, BLACK AND BELOVED

Hear me, Heed me, my beautiful black and beloved.
Wherever you are and whatever your station.
Be you blue collar, or white collar, or no collar.
Listen.

Black Jesuses in steel mills and stock yards
Black geniuses sorting and carrying mail
Black madonnas residing heavenwise
Black runners to the corner pub
Young black scrawlers on ghetto walls
Listen.

All of you beautiful, and black beloved;
I want to talk to you, about you, and me and us
About our black selves, a glory people.

I wish to speak of image, of black image
I wish to speak of beauty, of black beauty
To show you how beautiful our black people are
I want to smash your mirror reflecting alien vision
An image not akin to you, which causes you to reject
Your own very best and beautiful self.

I want to make you proud of your satin ebony skin
And the wiry crispness of your strong black hair
Or the rounded flaring of your nostrils
Or the expressive fullness of your lips
Or the large dark pools that are your eyes
And the lithesome grace of your athletic bodies.

I want you to be aware of the gifts of black folk
To this the new world and the entire world
Of how you beautiful and black beloved
Gave profound meaning to the word religion
Enriched a barren land with music and rhythm
Set unmatched model for generosity, kindness
Discipline, endurance, hope and self control;
Courage, bravery and compassion.

I want you to know these things about yourselves
About us, to truly know them and believe them
To spread this word to all black sisters and brothers
To counter the hateful racist propaganda,
With these truths to imbue your black generations.

And above all my beautiful black and beloved
To cleave together in unity all as part of a whole
And to love each other and work together
So that our black people may become
As DuBois the sage says, our own very best selves.

Margaret T. G. Burroughs

THE INCEPTION OF THE NEGRO

The Massa say it was a good thing what I did
    cause the food my Momma stole was rightly his.

He say I had no other choice than to tell
    that my Daddy hid them papers in the ole water
      well.

He say I'm a good little nigger; that my soul can be
      saved . . .
    if I out my heathen ways before I'm called to my
      grave.

I want to be good for my Massa Colonel Jim . . .
    as for my Momma and Daddy, don't want to be like
      them.

Besides, they dead; my Momma was cut in her belly,
    my Daddy hung from a tree . . .

    Too bad they wasn't good niggers, more like me.

Joe Nell Rice

EPILOGUE from PURLIE VICTORIOUS

A BENEDICTION

. . . Tonight, my friends —
I find, in being black, a thing of beauty:
A joy; a strength; . . . a secret cup of gladness;
A native land in neither time nor place —
A native land in every Negro face!

Be loyal to yourself: your skin; your hair;
Your lips, your Southern speech, your laughing kindness —
Are Negro kingdoms, vast as any other!

Accept in full the sweetness of your blackness —
Not wishing to be white, nor red, nor yellow:
Nor any other race, or face, but this.

Farewell my deep and Africanic brothers,
Be brave, keep freedom in the family,
Do what you can for the white folks,
And write me in care of the Post Office.

Now may the Constitution of the United States go with you;
the Declaration of Independence stand by you; the Bill of
Rights protect you; and the State Commission Against
Discrimination keep the eyes of the law upon you, henceforth,
now and forever.

Amen

Ossie Davis

BY THE WAY POLITICAL

I REMEMBER WHEN

I use to Die (D — I — E)
I use to straighten my hair
have a permanent
wear a wig ——let.
Use to study "glamor" "seventeen"
and "mademoiselle"
Use to use eye-liner —— daily
use to think I was hip
swingin' with brothers with
"good" hair
      straight hair
      curly hair
      no hair . . . .
but not "bad" hair.
I use to think "zero"
until I began to live . . . .
Get my mind
Got my natural ——
exchanged "seventeen"
for "wretched of the earth"
Stopped putting on my face
and started putting in my head.
I haven't always thought and
looked as I do.
I said before "I use to die"
clarification . . .
I use to be dead.

Bobby Alexander
Clarence Smith
Gwendolyn Williams
New Rochelle, H.S.

ON CONTEMPORARY ISSUES

Critical look?

I ain't takin'
No critical look
at nothin'
baby —
Cause what I see
Ain't hittin'
on a damn thing
anyway
You dig?

Critical?
What that mean?

Ridhiana

GO ON

Pop Dat Pill
Plunge Dat Needle
Pluck Dat Baby
Pull Dat Trigger.

Peep it, Baby
Peoples isn't Necessary
Nohow.

Ann Wallace

AN ARTIST ISN'T

An artist isn't a leader he's a pointer toward hope.

Gordon Nelson

A TRYING BLACK MAN

Brothers and Sisters
First of all, I'd like to say
Power to the People
I'll tell you, jim
I've tried to tell our people
Of many of the Injustices
We, as Black people have been evolving in
In this country

I've also tried to warn my people
Of the many traps that the white man
uses to suppress us.
But would they listen to Me?
No.

I've tried to set an example
By keeping myself physically strong
Mentally awake, and morally straight.

Well at least I know that I'm together
And when the revolution comes
I'll know about it.
God damn it — I ain't stupid.
I watch the six o'clock news.

Calvin Anderson
New Rochelle H.S.

BUYING MY ANGELA DAVIS POSTER

Buying my Angela Davis poster
She's not a person no more
   She's a martyr
     a revolutionary
     a beautiful sister
     and just another person dead in jail
   Alive among the dead
I'm gonna put her picture in my room.
   That dollar I spent will go to her defense fund —
      Part of it at least!

A lot of good money's gonna do her.
   Sitting in jail.

Waiting for her friends to free her,
   Waiting

What else can she do but sit and wait.

   I'm really gonna groove on this poster, man,
     Groove, what?

Groove myself
   Sho ain't gonna do Angela no good.

Gordon Nelson

JUST ASKED

What candidate ever ran
on a law and order ticket
to curb the Ku Klux Klan?

Ruth Duckett Gibbs

ABOUT VIETNAM

How much respect do you have for someone's
dead son killed in someone else's civil war?

Gordon Nelson

YOU CAN'T SHAKE HANDS WITH A FIST

You can't shake hands with a fist.
You can't have peace with war.
    You can't see people through mist.
You can't come close if you're far.
    You can't cure a gun-wound with
    a band-aid.
You can't stop hatred with a plea
    You can't help people if they're
    afraid.
Oh, won't someone listen to me?

Debbie Whitely
Albert Leonard Jr. H.S.

QUERY

All this moon jive may have its worth.
But when we gonna get down to earth?

Alfred Duckett

OH SAY, CAN YOU SEE

"Oh say, can you see
By the dawn's early light?"

   OF COURSE NOT

There's too much smog, fog, wog,
bog and other rough stuff that
cuts off my vision.

Ricky Smith
Albert Leonard Jr. H.S.

CAN I GET A AMEN?

"Love it or leave it."
Signs on cars and trucks say.
Imo make my own sign:
"Change it or lose it some day."

Alfred Duckett

Imo: Ghetto slang for "I'm going to".

AMERICAN BRAND REALITY

American brand Reality
    Look for Uncle Sam on the label
The more you swallow
    The more stars you see
The more you buy
    The bigger and better the stripes seem to become

Half-price-off special on independence day

If you can't find our product in your neighborhood

    Send Twenty-five cents and any Nixon Campaign button to

    Sorryful State
    Washington D.C.

    For your free catalog
        Life in the Black Ghetto and other fun Cocktail
        Party Subjects

Gordon Nelson

CITY HAPPENINGS

STREET PEOPLE

Black Persons of the asphalt
Stray Persons, a lost race
Without a home, never the same place
Running the sidewalks, Climbing the buildings
Masters of the rooftops My dear
Are you falling
My dear brother
Steam rises from sidewalks
Simmering
Sizzling
Suffocating
Black and Dark
Good and Dark
My dear
We are the Happy Street People
From the bottom of the gutter
to the top of the church steeple

But are we really of the streets?
Are we of the streets?
Have we been steamrolled
And baked
or
Cement mixed?
Someone said I had a black top
I'm insulted
When somebody says I'm a street person
Ain't nothing on the street but dirt
And you know I ain't dirt

Gordon Nelson

SEND ME A LETTER

If you got a letter coming my way
Get down with the nitty
Don't write New York City
Address it to me in Harlem, U.S.A.

It's a city within a city.
It's a compound.
It's Black town.
It's the home of frustration.
Black capitol of the nation.
It's a Black bank president and a Black guard guarding
It's a teen-age Brother in the hallway, junkie-nodding
It's folks up tight and in a lurch.
It's majestic Abyssinia Baptist Church.
It's the Apollo Theatre with lines around the block.
It's an early Saturday morning wino with a radio to hock.
It's chit'lins and fat back and a subway's black mouth.
It's relatives with suitcases coming up from the South.
It's the Lindsay walk.
It's a garbage-gutted street.
It's hipsters on street corners digging pigmeat.
Harlem's walk-up flats and non-rent-paying rats.
It's beautiful cats and sisters sweet.
It's a corner bar juke box with the loud down home beat.
It's Saturday night.
A stabbing fight.
The death chord in an emergency ward.
It's a white rookie cop saluting a black sarge.
It's a Black Borough President-in-charge.
Riding from the Terrace in his long limousine.
Checking out the political scene.
Harlem's hustling and heaving-black, bad and way over 21.
It's stickball and basketball and balling and fun.
It's a place of lovers and beloved as well.

It's a piece of heaven and a slice of hell. It's better than
   it has been, not good as it will be.
It's a plantation but the slaves are learning to be free.
Harlem's brutal and human.
It's a man and his woman.
A girl and her boy.
Harlem's brash and Harlem's coy.
Harlem hearts are kind but the outside core of Harlem is hard
   because Harlem is at war.
Cruel war within itself. War to keep alive.
To maintain its cool, its dignity. War to survive.
Harlem is foul and Harlem is fine.
Whatever it is Harlem is mine.
You pushed me off to this walled island.
And I'll make it a glorious kingdom — my land.

   So if you've got a letter coming my way —
   Get down with the nitty
   Don't write New York City.
   Address it to me in Harlem, U.S.A.

Alfred Duckett

A WELFARE MOTHER

Hide.
Here comes my caseworker
I've got to find a bed
No heat, no hot water,
Roaches in the bread
Five kids to feed and
All I got is twenty-five dollars a head.

Hide.
My caseworker is due
I've got to buy some shoes
No heat, no hot water,
Roaches in the bread
Ceiling peeling, bathroom flooding
Five kids crying, all in one bed.

Hide.
The caseworker is coming
I've got to find a man
No heat, no hot water,
Roaches in the bread
My man done gone
He got damn tired of
Hiding under the bed.

Glenn Hines

MOTHER'S DAY IN HARLEM

Mother's Day
Comes
Not in May
Not once a year
Here
In Harlem U.S.A.

Mother's Day
Is the day
Of welfare dole
When being soul
Costs more
In supermart
And corner store

Some babes get
Shoes
Some folks
Get Booze

Alfred Duckett

MOMMY I WENT FOR A RIDE

Mommy, I went for a ride in a white man car today.
He drove me home from school. His car is nice. It's real
big and soft. White people car sho do smell nice. Daddy
car smell funky, doesn't it. White mans car sho don't smell
like that. White man windows go up by it's self that's cool.
White man sho is nice give us candy and we sang songs. White
man sho is funny. He told me some jokes. He sho do have a
nice car, Daddy's car is stinky. Daddy should get a white
mans car. Why doesn't Daddy get a white mans car. I wish
I were old enough to buy the white mans car. I wish I
were White.

White people are happy aren't they Mommy?

Gordon Nelson

MICHIGAN AUTUMN

detroit's not a bad
place to grow up in
if u don't know
other places exist
seasons come n tarry
bringing with them the
freshness of change
when fall came
it didn't quite matter
to us
if there was no electricity
or if the plumbing had broken down
it didn't really matter
if we had only moth-eaten secondhand sweaters
n thin-soled sneakers to brave the onrushing cold
for we had grown
to accept these conditions
as the natural order of things
unaware
we didn't know the rest of the wld existed
n though happy by default
we squeezed every bit of joy
out of our cornered existence
we would rake leaves into heaping piles
n crackle them under our feet
n our dog joined in
n scampered thru pile after pile
of neighbors' leaves
as she followed us to
the after school football game
we'd hurl our young bodies
thru the cool still air
that chapped our lips

n turned our skins an ashen gray
n bash each other
to the ground
like young gladiators
as we played out the last innocent
moments of our lives
when the awesome autumn sun
turned the western skies red
n slipped behind grand blvd
the boundary of our wld
we'd trek home
to be greeted by the wild erotic incense
of burning leaves
all along the block/like beacons
to guide weary travelers
fiery leaves glowed
silhouetting figures of men with rakes
n children enchanted by flame
we'd postpone homework
to dip our fingers into
mason jars of plum/apple/n cherry jam
stored away for the winter
those were the mellow autumns
of the blissful years
before we embarked upon
our predestined journey
before we discovered
the outside wld
before we found that
cigarettes n cheap wine
n hastily issued promises of love
separated brown sugar mamas
from their chastity
before school turned sour
n made us hate / n fear the wld we didn't know
n ourselves
before bobby became a junkie

n bad wine drove j.d. crazy
before freckles gave up hope
n nicky became a faggot
before the girls were
cursed with the fruits of nature
n subjected themselves to
hack butchers / or foul social workers
before we discovered
other things / n other places
autumn n michigan was hip

Othello Mahome

LOVE YOUR ENEMY

Brought here in slave ships and pitched over board.
Love your enemy.

Language taken away, culture taken away.
Love your enemy.

Work from sun-up to sun-down.
Love your enemy.

Work for no pay.
Love your enemy.

Rape your mother.
Love your enemy.

Lynch your father.
Love your enemy.

Bomb your churches.
Love your enemy.

Force to fight his wars.
Love your enemy.

Pay the highest rent.
Love your enemy.

Sell you rotten foods.
Love your enemy.

Sell dope to your children.
Love your enemy.

Forced to live in slums.
Love your enemy.

Dilapidated schools.
Love your enemy.

Puts you in jail.
Love your enemy.

Bitten by dogs.
Love your enemy.

Water-hose you down.
Love your enemy.
    Love.
    Love.
    Love.
    Love.
    Love.
    Love, for everybody else.
But when will we love ourselves?

Yusef Iman

FIRST PARADOX

The final cop-out
A syringe and
A pulsating vein
Coke, scag and
A thousand reefers
Burning on a
Junk sick morning
Blue crystals being
Snorted and sniffed
Into a raw nose
Damp, sunless morning
Slime and pus oozing
Out of an infected
Vein
Sticking needles into
every point of
Contact
Oh God why can't I o.d.?
Scratching, scratching, scratching
Bloody hands
Streets of decaying bones
And tormented pecan nutmeg
Babies

Junk pushing in
On a junk
Sick morning
Death around every
Corner
Broken skulls and deteriorated
Flesh
Swollen hands and ashy-grey
Faces
Transitions in rhythms of
Withdrawal
A burned-out brain
On a junk sick
Morning.

Glenn Hines

PEOPLE HAVE TOLD ME

People have told me that I'm a punk
    Inexperienced, you know
I just act too young for their crowd
      I'm a kid
   They are mature, you see
   More mature than me.
Hip,
   That brother sitting over there smoking pot
He's a man
   That sister over there begging someone to sleep
      with her tonight
She's a woman

    See, me
  I have a goal, my line is straight
Me, I'm a punk, a kid.

Brothers and Sisters, I can always grow
      But you can't erase.

Gordon Nelson

TWO LITTLE BOYS

Have you seen the skinny little boy
That chases the white ghosts at night?
Face puffed up/tracks in his arm and his mind blown
His momma somewhere drinking
And talking about survival
Pops in jail or downtown at the Y.
The little boy chases the white ghost with his friend
And they get high? And they get high
Like cloud nine
Where everything is fine

Have you seen two little boys running past you
With a lady's purse?
They stole a Black woman's purse
The other day
Yesterday/today/tomorrow
Face puffed up
Tracks in their arm
Eyes popping out of their skulls
And their minds blown
And they get high/and they get high
Talkin' 'bout trippin'/talkin' 'bout flyin'
Talkin' 'bout getting high? Gettin' high

Have you seen two little boys sitting in Sylvia's
Stuffing chicken and cornbread down their tasteless mouths?
Trying to revive a dying heart
Shrinking lungs and wasted minds
Have you seen the sickness of our people?

And all the while we parade around
In robes of our ancestors
And wisdoms of the universe
And all the while there are children dying
Chasing the white ghost
Whitey is dying and his fucking ghost is killing us
Oh beautiful Black hands
Reach out and snatch the death out of the youth of our
        nation
Oh beautiful Black minds
Create, create the world for children to play with life
And not with death
Oh beautiful Black brothers and sisters
Come together and create life
Come together and create love
Come together and create, create
Come together and create, create

Abiodun Oyewole

TO A YOUNG BLOOD

Quit hanging on the corner, man . . .
Just because you're late, black boy!
Stop waiting, blood, to be released
From feeling like YOU'RE the worthless one,
Picked on by other folks . . .
Whenever they feel out-of-sorts.
Man! . . . refuse to be crushed!
A new tomorrow is yours,
Stop trying to be a cool fool . . .
Let sunshine through the windows
Of your soul.

Quit hanging on the corner, man . . .
Get off the orange crate, black boy!
Stop sitting there with your pants creased
And your cheap watch shining in the sun,
Digging on other folks . . .
As they cruise by in their fine shorts
Leaving you in the dust . . .
Squinting through those shades of yours
That you think make you look so cool . . .
Just by hiding the windows
Of your soul.

Quit hanging on the corner, man . . .
You've got a big date, black boy!
Stop acting like you're the least
Of all God's children under the sun,
Capping on other folks . . .
With your hip words and sly retorts
Full of hate and distrust . . .
Frowning through those tints of yours
That you sport when you're ditching school . .
To hide the frightened windows
Of your soul.

Quit hanging on the corner, man . . .
You've got to face fate, black boy!
Stop bumming from west to east
And vice-versa . . . always on the run,
Hitting on other folks . . .
Just because you refuse to start
Thinking the way you must!
Take off those dark shades of yours
Don't just grow up to be a fool . . .
Man! . . . open up the windows
Of your soul!

Blossom Powe

THE MORNING COMING IN

I saw the morning coming in and
All the butterflies whirled and spun
Their colors in a kaleidoscope dream
And the air was alive
With wind and music
And barefoot people running
Through the grass
Coming and going
Mixing with the sun
That screamed its name
And made the flowers jump
And the birds yell
And love was all around
Crying and killing
Soulin' and living
And calling stones out of their bag
Telling them to live
And be
And grow
Soft like skin
Hot and cold and
Gentle
And love was so beautiful that it hurt
And hurt drifted away and left me
With the morning I saw coming in

Dorothy Randall

YOU CAN TELL ME

"Tell me, little brother!
"Tell me confidentially.
When you smashed the pawnshop window
and copped that color tv,
did you go to all that trouble
just so black folks could be free?

Tell me, little brother —

or you just like tv?"

Alfred Duckett

FACE IT

No matter how
dippy bop
you walk . . .

Or how hard
you
street corner talk . . .

Brown boy.
Black boy.
You know better
than any other
that jail
with no bail
is a very
tough
mother!

Alfred Duckett

THE BEAT

This is about the size of it, Dad.
Time just hasn't done, for me, the things
You said it would.
It's been a bad scene all the way 'round.
Like you told me to play it cool — wait for the happenings.
And I said, "Yeah."
So I just dug the sounds.
Old Life rolled squeaking out of Prez's horn
And Lady Day came on.
Yardbird squealed the hurt and I dug it all.
And cooled it.
But those cats were just like me, Dad.
They weren't moving.
Not really into anything.
They knew the bad deal and spat it out on wax.
But they weren't going anyplace.
Somehow I've had it, Baby, up to here.
The main sounds, now, come floating out of Malcolm's ax —
Stokely and Rap sit in as side men.
And little shriveled up Jimmy Baldwin's phrase
Is telling it like it is: "God gave Noah the Rainbow sign.
      No more water — the fire next time."
I got to get with it, Dad.
I got to make it — on this set . . .

James R. Lucas

WISDOM, HOPE, GOD

THE TREE

In the beginning God planted
a seed
and it was a beautiful
Black seed
and the fruit of the seed
was life
and to the coldness of
the earth
the seed brought a
beautiful
     black
        energy/life/force
and the fruit from the seed
grew into strong black
warrior kings
and beautiful black
gentle queens
and from this fruit
came the seeds
of the nation
   of beautiful
     black
honor and
   truth
But the devil, being the
natural enemy
   of God
could not stand the beauty
of his work
and so sent his children.
to maim
   and destroy
The tree of blackness
The tree of life

And so began four hundred years
for the children
        of God
in the land
    of the devil
four hundred years
    of physical and
    mental slavery
four hundred years
    of insult
    after insult
    atrocity after
    atrocity

And black leaders rose and fell
Rose in the spirit of blackness
and fell by the hands
        of the devil
And Nat Turner rose and
        fell
And Marcus Garvey rose and
        fell
And Malcolm X rose and
        fell
And Martin Luther King rose and
        fell
and the dream fell
and the segregated people
separated
Then the righteous people
realized
that the devil couldn't
help them

And thoughts of the nation rise
        but will not fall
Because we must have
        our souls
we must have
        our lives
we must have
        our righteousness
we will have
        our nation
and once again
The Tree will be
as one.

Frederick Crawley

THE POET SPEAKS

I know there seems to be
Little reason or rhyme
For poets who write of beauty
In such conflicting times . . .
But I am one of those
Who strive to yield,
Golden fruits, from stone fields.

John Henrik Clarke

TODAY IS OURS

Today is ours; let's live it.
And love is strong; let's give it.
A song can help; let's sing it.
And peace is dear; let's bring it.
The past is gone; don't rue it.
Our work is here; let's do it.
Our world is wrong; let's right it.
The battle hard; let's fight it.
The road is rough; let's clear it.
The future vast; don't fear it.
Is faith asleep? let's wake it.
Today is ours; let's take it!

Author Unknown

THE IZES OF LIFE

Mankind?
   He be christianized
Religion?
   It be organized
Society?
   That be stylized
Life be full of . . . *izes*
Food be merchandized
Work
   Mechanized
Science
   Computerized
And Black minds?
They be
   Hypnotized!
      Hyp-no-tized!
         Hip not . . . . ized!

Greg Russell

LESS MAJESTE

No matter how high or great the throne,
What sits on it is the same as your own.

E.Y. Harburg

PRAY

PRAY!
    What's the matter with you?
    You sick or something?

PRAY!
    Come off it, man!

PRAY!
    You gotta be kidding.

PRAY!

Carl F. Burke

C'MON NOW

Love, Love, Let's Say "I love".
A great sound to be puttin' down.
Soul Sound
Mole Sound — Dig?
Not just for holes in the ground or
Ditches for pipes and wires and sewers or
Foundations.
Dig love
Dig unwar — all *over* forever
Dig those that got it inside, outside.
    Those that *don't* got it
Dig bread for everybody
Loving people we don't even know.
Dig *out* burrs on the brain that
    Make us lie to ourselves or make us
Hate somebody or kill somebody or
Make us sick or
DRIVE US CRAZY!
Let's bite the apple 'til we get to the core.
Fight the battle 'til we get to the sore.
Let's understand — numbers, nonsense,
Friends, beauty
Fatheads and saints —
C'mon —
Let's do a mind grind
Like the mole in the hole and dig
Deeper 'til we get clear through to the
Other side of most everything and then
MAKE THAT SOUND!
What Sound?
Soul Sound — say "I love"
DO THAT THING!
Like the mole in the hole and dig —
Understand? Dig. Dig.

Ann Wallace

THE MEETING

Yes, he turned and he walked
Past the eyes of my life
And he nodded and sang
Without sound.
And his face had the look
Of a man who knew strife
And a feeling familiarly
Came around
I said

CHORUS:
Man — Where have you been for all these years
Man — Where were you, when I sought you
Man — Do you know me as I know you
Man — Am I coming through?

And he spoke in a voice
That was centuries old
And he smiled in a way
That was strange
And his full lips of night
Spoke about our people's plight
And a feeling familiarly
Came around
I said

CHORUS:
And we sat and we talked
About freedom and things
And he told me about
What he dreamed
But I knew of that dream
Long before he had spoken
And a feeling familiarly
Came around
I said

CHORUS

Elaine Brown

CAN MEN ONE DAY LIVE

Can men one day live
without the dominating need
to crush another
to prove their worth
as a person

    or a nation?

Can we grow a person
to know his own worth
within himself?
Does he need to dominate
another, put down another,
Kill another
to prove his value to himself
and his friends?

"Religion
is the answer!
Faith in God,
and organized religion
is the answer!"

"Which one?"
"The True one!"
"Which one?"
    A thousand voices from different
    churches and organized religions
    shout! . . .

"THIS ONE!"

Donald S.C. Davis

GOD!

My face is red,
My ears are black,
My nose is orange & blue,
My hair is green,
My eyes opaline,
My toes a purplish hue,
My mind is yellow,
My teeth are brown,
I am all colors at once,
For I am GOD . . . and GOD
doesn't rhyme.

Gary Feldman
Albert Leonard Jr. H.S.

SPELLED BACKWARDS

L – O – V – E.
The beginning of
Evolution.

L – O – V – E – R.
The beginning of
Revolution.

Anonymous

TREAT ME COOL, LORD
(A Litany for Others)

God, help us give a care for others
    We ask your help.
For those what got kicked out of their houses
    We ask your help.
For those what fight for us
    We ask your help.
For those who ain't got no job
    We ask your help.
For those who give up too soon
    We ask your help.
For those who think that clothes is everything
    We ask your help.
For those who are always bugged by others
    We ask your help.
For those who just hang around
    We ask your help.
For those who need to try harder
    We ask your help.
For those who think they know it all
    We ask your help.
But don't know as much as they think
    We ask your help.
For those who think we are dirt
    We ask your help.
Help us, God, to give a care.

Carl F. Burke

IN THE BEGINNING

In The Beginning, God created the world, and in the
world he created the birds, the flowers, the trees, sky,
sun, moon, grass, and all other things which make you laugh
when you're in love, and make you cry when you're alone.

Then God created Man and Woman. When they met, Man brought
his Strength, Speed, Woman brought Softness, gentleness,
God brought wisdom. They all sat down on the damp, sweet
grass and talked and communicated and loved. Until a snake
appeared, slithered up and wiggled down and thought evil
thoughts. Snake brought his radio tuned to WWRL turned up
to full volume. Snake dressed up in snake-skin suit,
alligator shoes, irridescent bow-tie and apple-jack leather.
Man and Woman turned inside out, dug this turned-inside-out
music. Snake said "dig it", and they dug it. Snake said
"let's party, baby," and they partied, and they partied
and they partied.

Forty days and Forty nights after God created the World and
God created Man and Woman, Man and Woman were still partying.
Man brought Strength, Speed, Dope, Porkchops, Beer. Woman
brought Softness, Gentleness, Potato Salad, Greens.

Man was dressing fly. Woman was dressing fly. Miniskirts
and high-heeled boots. Snake brought his radio tuned to
WWRL turned all the way up to full volume. Snake said
"Let's party." They said "yeah, we partying." And they
partied, and partied, and they partied, and they partied,
to this very day. I'm digging it brother.

Gordon Nelson

ANXIETY

I am not afraid of
Gray hair,
or wrinkled hands
But of an old mind.

Norman Jordan

PEACE AND FREEDOM

A SONG OF PEACE

Across the mountains and the beaches
I hear the cries of the children
    laughing
    leaping
    running
They climb the sun ladder
they clean the clouds of danger
  They make the earth
cleaner than it ever was.
  In their multitudes
each one is a star
  creating a world that can love.

(From "The Sioux" in Thou Shalt Not Overkill*).*

UNITY

How can we be unified
When our thoughts and wants
Are so diversified?
If I love you and
You love me
We don't have to always
Agree
I'll try to find out what makes you tick
Why you go the way you go
Do the things you do
Then you try the same for
Me.
We just can't give up on each other.
It's the trying that makes us
Sister and brother.
If we can't try with another
Human being
Then this world is not where we belong
In unity there is power and strength
But it's the striving toward unity
That makes us strong.

Anonymous

WHEN

When will I stop hearing violins
and hear only drums.

When will I stop seeing grey
and only see colors.

When will I stop hearing scratches
and only hear music.

When will I stop being two
and only be one.

When will I stop feeling half
and start feeling whole.

When will I stop saying tomorrow
and start saying now.

When will I stop trying
and start doing.

When will I stop crying
and start laughing.

When will I stop humming
and start singing.

When will I stop thinking
and start loving.

When will I be free, when, when . . .

Rakeman

FREE AS A BIRD

A bird flies
Free
It is also
Bound
To branches of trees
To worms
To other birds.
A ball knows
Freedom
Fleeing from a hand
Or blasted by a bat
And snatched at by gravity
A people know
Freedom
Only when they are
Bound
To a strong idea
Living a life
Dedicated to its fulfillment.

Ann Wallace

GUY DAVIS POEM

Across the vast great plains
Over Blue mountain tops stretching the
sky —
We search — we search — oh —
We sip the waters from the lakes of life
We hold our faces up to the sun.
Then soaring up to the stars
Where the fountains of night
Bathe our souls
  We are free.

Guy Davis

SO MUCH OF ME

So much of me
Wants to be free —
From the foulness of life
To dance and laugh and love.
So I'll chain my life to beauty
And beat my way to truth
I'll fight white evil and colorless death
Root out black sorrow and
Dam the flow of
Red blood out of place and
Fill hungry bellies and
Calm fearful vacant hearts.
I only hope that
Beauty's chain is strong.

Ann Wallace

PEACE

On old copy books
    on my school desk on treetops
       I write your name.

On all pages
    anyone ever read
. . . .

    I write your name.

On jungles
    on deserts
On eagle's nests
    on echoes of my childhood
      I write your name.

On the marvels of night
on the day's bread
on seasons that love one another.
    I write your name.
On my faded-blue rags
    on the musty pool of the sun
      on the living lake of the moon
        I write your name.

On fields across the horizon
    on wings of birds
On shadows behind the mill
    I write your name.
On every puff of dawn
    on the sea on ships
On crazy mountain tops
    I write your name.

. . . .
On footpaths that wake up
    on highways that branch out
        on public squares that are flowing over
    I write your name.

. . . .
On that fruit cut in half
On my bedroom mirror and my bedroom
        on the empty shell of my bed
    I write your name.

On my greedy and affectionate dog
    on his perked-up ears
        and his limp awkward paw
    I write your name.

On the springboard of my door
    on every common object
        on the top flame of the fire
    I write your name.
    on my friends' foreheads
On each body I love
        on every outstretched hand
    I write your name.

. . . .
On absence without loving
    on loneliness behind bars
        on the stairway to death
    I write your name.

On health won back
   on danger passed
      on baseless hope
   I write your name.

And by the weight of one word
   I start my life over again
I was born to know you
      and call you by your name
      PEACE!

Paul Eluard

This Book is set in 10 point Press Roman with Press Roman Bold display. It is printed on 60 Basis Danforth paper and has a Reinforced Binding, covered with Crown Linen cloth.

Was set by Live Gold Productions Inc., New York City, and printed and bound by The Maple Press Company, York, Pennsylvania.

Designed by Ben Arrington